FREECOUVER

101 free things to do in & around Vancouver

JOHN LEE & REBECCA BOLLWITT

TIDEWATER
PRESS

DISCLAIMER: To the best of our knowledge, the information contained in this book was correct at time of writing. However, things change and specifics may alter. If you are unsure about any of the attractions or experiences, we recommend contacting them directly to confirm the current details.

Published by Tidewater Press
New Westminster, BC, Canada
tidewaterpress.ca

978-1-990160-75-2 (print)
978-1-990160-76-9 (e-book)

Photographs by Rebecca Bollwitt, miss604.com, and John Lee
Cover photograph of fridge by Nerthuz@istockphoto.com
Freecouvering maps based on Vancouver Area Map from vectormap.net

LIBRARY AND ARCHIVES CANADA CATALOGUING IN PUBLICATION
Title: Freecouver : 101 free things to do in & around Vancouver / John Lee & Rebecca Bollwitt.
Names: Lee, John, 1969- author. | Bollwitt, Rebecca, author.
Identifiers: Canadiana (print) 20260188603 | Canadiana (ebook) 20260189642 | ISBN 9781990160752 (softcover) | ISBN 9781990160769 (EPUB)
Subjects: LCSH: Vancouver Metropolitan Area (B.C.)—Guidebooks. | LCGFT: Guidebooks.
Classification: LCC FC3847.18 .L432 2026 | DDC 917.11/33045—dc23

Canada

Tidewater Press gratefully acknowledges the support of the Government of Canada.

Contents

WELCOME TO FREECOUVER

It's easy to give up on going out when you live in a city routinely described as one of the most expensive in Canada. But rather than staying on our couches and admitting defeat, we've taken a different approach: scouting out and visiting the very best free attractions and activities in and around Vancouver.

In the process, we unearthed a huge array of museums, gardens, galleries, tours and more that welcome your patronage without draining your dollars. Many are hidden gems and all are ideal for locals or visitors searching for budget-friendly alternatives. We've only included places and experiences where admission is free. However, you'll likely spot donation boxes at many locations—this is a great way to be extra supportive and help to keep these experiences free for all.

More than half of the listed attractions are located in Vancouver, with the rest dotted throughout the Lower Mainland. While a car might be handy for reaching some, we discovered our excellent transit system connects you to almost everything—TransLink's Trip Planner (at *translink.ca*) was our constant companion throughout this project.

We've categorized our entries into themes. So if you're in the mood for Museums & History (M&H), Arts & Entertainment (A&E) or Gardens & Nature (G&N) you can easily browse your options via our user-friendly labelling system. We have higlighted attractions that offer dedicated children's programming as Great for Kids (GFK). Each entry lists other attractions nearby in case you want to combine multiple experiences for a full day out. While the information in this book was correct at time of writing, specifics may alter, so we've included QR codes that link directly to each attraction's website.

We believe that "Freecouvering"—the action of purposely visiting free places in and around our city—goes hand-in-hand with a slow travel approach. We fully endorse taking your time wherever you happen to be visiting: there's nothing to be gained by rushing! We've included several Freecouvering walks (with maps) that guide you around specific neighbourhoods, where you will find attractions that fit in all categories. We encourage you to slow down to a stately saunter and observe fascinating details such as historic plaques, art installations or architectural features you might otherwise not have noticed.

You'll also find some Freecouver Tips sprinkled throughout this book. These spotlight practical resources to help you plan your own budget-friendly activities. Additional advice and information—including a monthly list of free local events—is available on our website: *freecouver.com.*

We hope you have as much fun exploring Vancouver and the Lower Mainland as we did. And if you find any attractions or experiences you think would fit the bill for our next edition, let us know via our website. We'd love to hear about your fantastic Freecouver discoveries!

John & Rebecca

Throughout this book, we visited locations within the unceded territories of the Coast Salish Peoples who have stewarded this land since time immemorial. This includes the Sḵwx̱wú7mesh (Squamish), xʷməθkʷəy̓əm (Musqueam) and səlilwətaɬ (Tsleil-Waututh) Nations; the q̓icə̓y̓ (Katzie), q̓ʷɑ:n̓ƛ̓ən̓ (Kwantlen), and se'mya'me (Semiahmoo) Nations; Stó:lō, qiqéyt (Qayqayt) and Tsawwassen First Nations; and the kʷikʷəƛ̓əm (Kwikwetlem) First Nation. We recognize and respect their enduring connection to the land, waters and community, as well as their ongoing contributions to the cultural and social life of this region.

Many venues in this book feature Indigenous art, displays and cultural spaces, or have a history of hosting Indigenous-led exhibitions and a stated commitment to continuing this work. In the spirit of reconciliation, we encourage you to learn directly from cultural guides and leaders by paying tour and admission fees as you are able.

ATTRACTIONS BY CATEGORY

GARDENS & NATURE G&N

MUSEUMS & HISTORY M&H

ARTS & ENTERTAINMENT A&E

GREAT FOR KIDS GFK

VANCOUVER

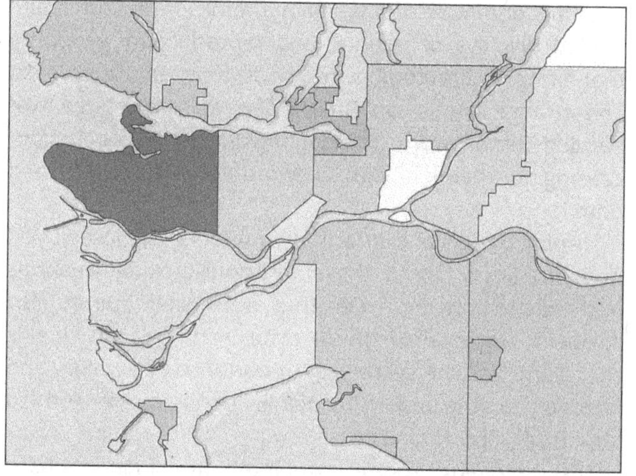

ACADEMIE DUELLO'S SWORDPLAY MUSEUM

M&H

GFK

412 West Hastings Street, Vancouver

Searching for Vancouver's bloodthirsty medieval side? Head to downtown's Academie Duello, where popular classes and workshops in historic European martial arts—from sword skills to axe throwing—are complemented by a fascinating, family-friendly museum that's open to anyone with even a passing interest in olde-worlde disembowelling techniques.

Lining one wall of the main room, you'll find multi-bladed displays of antique and reproduction weaponry that bring to life combat methods from centuries past. These range from a cool Bronze Age rapier to a huge two-handed broadsword to—our favourite—a concussion-causing pole hammer with its own cheeky little face etched onto it.

Display panels and information folders tell you all you need to know about these ferocious-looking weapons and exactly how and when they were used. There's also a kaleidoscopic array of colourful, hand-painted shields that illuminate the yesteryear importance of heraldry and lineage—aka the underlying nobility of ripping someone to shreds for a principled cause.

The adjoining room—complete with loaner board games and a café (don't miss their regular tavern nights)—has even more to offer, with longbows, arrows and a siege machine exhibit. Speaking of arrows, there's also a fully costumed Agincourt archer figure displayed here. If you're suddenly inspired to dress up like him, you'll find an inviting table of try-on helmets, gauntlets and chain mail nearby to help you unleash your inner medieval warrior.

Ready to take it to the next level? Academie Duello typically offers free trial classes.

Nearby

- B.C. Binning Mural (p. 3)
- Marine Building (p. 27)
- Freecouvering Around Chinatown (p. 6)

B.C. BINNING MURAL

A&E

586 Granville Street, Vancouver

Look up from the shelves of snacks and shampoo at this downtown Shoppers Drug Mart and you'll spot something that truly looks like it shouldn't be there. Dominating one of the store's second-level walls is a shimmering 13.5-metre-long modernist mosaic that's as vibrant as a Technicolor movie. It's time to abandon the Cheetos and climb the nearby staircase for a closer look.

Created by celebrated Canadian artist B.C. (Bertram Charles) Binning to adorn the interior of a bank that opened here in 1958, this eye-popping mural—crafted from around 200,000 Venetian glass tiles—depicts the province's main mid-century economic sectors. And while that might sound boring, the stylized nature of the work makes for a highly imaginative pictorial bristling with vivid details.

Each industry is portrayed with positivity and abundance. Look out for the fishing sector with its bulging net; farming with its oversized livestock; and forestry with its ready-to-chop surfeit of giant conifers. The financial markets are also depicted in a currency bar graph—although only dollars, francs and pounds seem to have been important at the time.

Our favourite details in this hidden-in-plain-sight art installation are the fruit sector—where the trees are laden with pears the size of soccer balls—and air transport, complete with a helicopter that looks like it was hybridized with a dragonfly. Take your time and find your own favourite features when you visit. Just don't forget to buy that all-important bag of Cheetos before you leave.

For more examples of B.C.'s Binning's work, head along Burrard Street. The former Dal Grauer Substation (at No. 944) and the old BC Electric Building (at No. 970) both feature exteriors created by the celebrated artist.

Nearby

- Academie Duello's Swordplay Museum (p. 2)
- BC Entertainment Hall of Fame
- StarWalk (p. 4)

BC ENTERTAINMENT HALL OF FAME STARWALK

A&E

Granville Street between Robson & Nelson Streets, Vancouver

Have a visit with Michael J. Fox, take a photo with Sarah McLachlan, enjoy lunch beside Michael Bublé and pose with Bryan Adams—all in bronze star-in-the-sidewalk form. These British Columbia icons have made a lasting impact on the entertainment industry, and you can find them on the BC Entertainment Hall of Fame StarWalk.

Since its founding in 1992, the BC Entertainment Hall of Fame has installed more than 200 bronze stars in the sidewalks here, celebrating the artists, dancers, musicians, impresarios, actors, directors and composers who have shaped the province's entertainment history.

This self-guided experience runs along both sides of Granville Street, beginning at either Robson Street to the north or Nelson Street to the south. As you stop to admire trailblazers such as Eleanor Collins, Canada's First Lady of Jazz, or Chief Dan George, the first North American Indigenous person nominated for an Academy Award, don't forget to look up. The glowing neon marquees of historic venues—the Orpheum, the Commodore Ballroom and the Vogue Theatre—still light up this storied stretch of Granville.

Inside the Orpheum Theatre lobby, brass plaques recognize other outstanding performers in a Standing Ovation exhibit. You'll need a show ticket or ticket to one of the monthly Orpheum Tours to view those. On Seymour Street off Smithe, by the Orpheum's stage door, you'll find Vancouver Favourites, a tribute to legendary performers including B.B. King, Bob Hope, Mitzi Gaynor and Harry Belafonte. These performers may not be British Columbians, but their local performances have been beloved by audiences through the years.

Nearby

- B.C. Binning Mural (p. 3)
- Contemporary Art Gallery (p. 11)

BC GOLF MUSEUM

M&H

2545 Blanca Street, Vancouver

Housed in the gabled former clubhouse of the University Golf Club, you don't have to be conversant with bogeys and five irons to enjoy this brilliantly eclectic little museum. Packed to the rafters with colourful exhibits and surprising artifacts, it fuses a social history approach to the sport with displays on its origins and growth.

That starts with "colf," first played on ice in the Netherlands in the 1400s before Scottish merchants moved it onto land in their own country. Check out the 500-year-old Dutch club heads here before perusing displays on golf's 19th-century arrival in BC. Soon, communities from Haney to Shaughnessy had their own courses and the game was often played in winter when the grass was at its lowest.

Exploring the cabinets, you'll find antique clubs, shiny trophies and golf-themed memorabilia ranging from vintage postcards to quirky club pins to a 1920s cookie tin. There's also a library bursting with browsable tomes (including a replica of 1743's first-ever golf book) and a hall of fame that celebrates BC players from Stan Leonard to Violet Sweeney and more.

Aiming for your own place in the hall of fame? You can even practice a few testers and tap-ins here. A free pitch-and-putt area was recently added just outside the museum and you're invited to bring your own club—ask nicely and they'll even loan you one—so you can tackle a few holes on the manicured green.

> **Freecouver Tip** Some paid attractions offer regular free, reduced price or pay-what-you-can days. Check our website for a complete list.

Nearby

- UBC Attractions (p. 45-51)
- Southlands Heritage Farm (p. 38)
- Pacific Spirit Regional Park (p. 32)

FREECOUVERING . . . AROUND CHINATOWN

One of the oldest and largest Chinatowns in Canada, this National Historic Site has architecture shaped by layered histories, bustling markets, unique shops and mouthwatering dining options. Start at the **Millenium Gate (1)** at 26 West Pender Street. Its ornamental arches reach across the road, marking the entrance to Chinatown and symbolizing a bridge between Orient and Occident, traditional and modern.

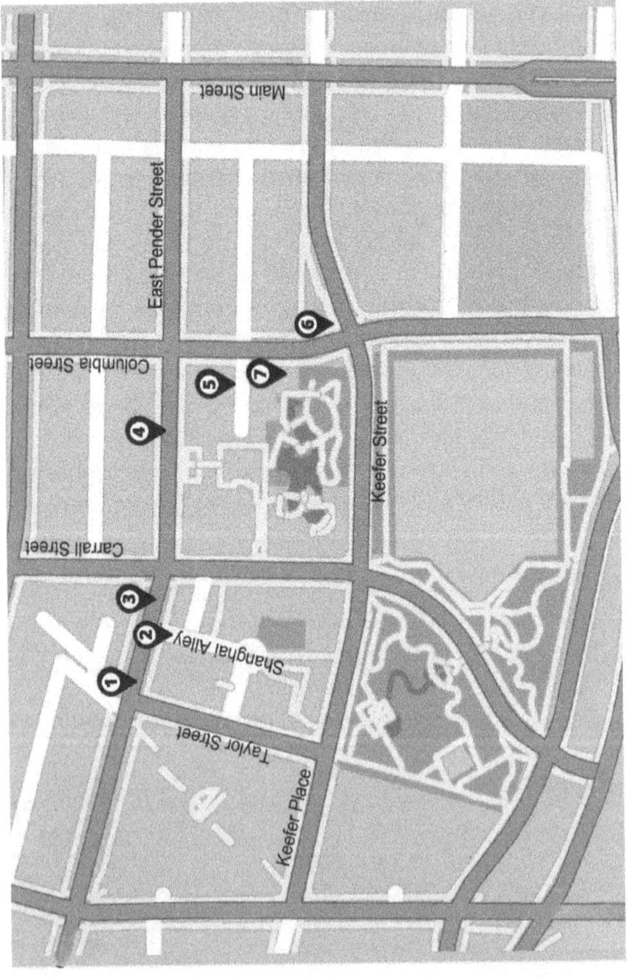

Continue along West Pender to **Shanghai Alley (2)**, a significant place in Chinatown history. In 2016, it was renamed Lilian To Way, becoming the first street in the city named after a Chinese Canadian. Walk down the alley to where it ends at a roundabout with a bell in the centre. This replica of a 2,200-year-old Western Han Dynasty bell was a gift from one of Vancouver's sister cities, Guangzhou.

Head back out to West Pender and spot the thinnest commercial building in the world, according to the *Guinness Book of Records*. The 1.6-metre-wide **Sam Kee Building (3)**—now Jack Chow Insurance—was built in 1913 and has a basement that extends under the sidewalk. Stretch out your hands and pose for a photo outside (there's an admission fee to get a closer look inside).

Cross Carrall Street, where West Pender turns into East Pender, to find the oldest building in Chinatown, the recently renovated **Wing Sang Building (4)** at 51 East Pender Street. Built in 1889 by merchant Yip Sang, it is now home to the Chinese Canadian Museum (admission fees apply here). Continue along East Pender to Columbia and turn south to the **Chinese Cultural Centre of Vancouver (5)**. Admission is free, with donations appreciated, if you have an opportunity to look around their museum and cultural exhibitions.

Across the street on the corner of Columbia and Keefer is the **Chinatown Memorial Monument (6)** with two bronze figures: one represents a railway worker, recognizing the thousands of Chinese Canadians who lived and died building the Canadian Pacific Railway that connected the country in the decades following Confederation; the other is a Chinese Canadian soldier, representing Chinese Canadians who volunteered to serve in the Second World War. End your tour at the gated **Dr Sun Yat-Sen Public Park (7)**. This serene oasis provides a free glimpse into the beautiful Dr. Sun Yat-Sen Classical Chinese Garden (paid admission). The park is operated by the City of Vancouver and opening hours may vary.

Nearby

- Freecouvering Around Gastown (p. 18)
- Academie Duello's Swordplay Museum (p. 2)

CHRIST CHURCH CATHEDRAL

M&H

690 Burrard Street, Vancouver

If the sandwich board sign is out and the doors are open, which is usually any weekday, everyone is welcome to visit Christ Church Cathedral in downtown Vancouver.

The first iteration of the cathedral was built of granite quarried from **Little Mountain Quarry Gardens (p. 35)**; the current sandstone building, completed in 1895, is still the oldest church building in the city. It's not just architecture buffs who will admire the Gothic Revival-style hammerbeam trusses, cedar tongue-and-groove ceiling and dozens of stained-glass windows. Don't forget to turn around and spot the 2,500-pipe organ.

Memorial plaques date back to the incorporation of the city, with particular tributes to Frederick Seymour, governor of BC; and Henry John Cambie, chief surveyor of the CPR's Pacific Division, who orchestrated construction of the church. Streets and buildings bear the names of both men; Seymour is also the namesake of one of the North Shore Mountains. Among the storied heritage elements, a QR code on the wall near the "Windows Dedicated to Women" will open a Spotify audio tour on your mobile. The earliest windows were installed in 1909 and include memorials to those who died in the First and Second World Wars. Recent additions include Musqueam artist Susan Point's *Tree of Life* window (2013).

On the way out, visitors are encouraged, but not required, to make a donation via a tap board. Visit the Hillman Garden along the west side of the building with fountains and a large Celtic cross.

To the east, between the Bill Reid Gallery and Cathedral Place, there's an excellent view of the stained-glass bell tower installed during the cathedral's renovations in 2016. Chimes ring at 8:00 am and 6:00 pm daily.

Nearby

- Fairmont Hotel Vancouver Museum (p. 22)
- Pendulum Gallery (p. 33)
- Contemporary Art Gallery (p. 11)

CITY FARMER DEMONSTRATION GARDEN

G&N

2150 Maple Street, Vancouver

Recently awarded a Places That Matter heritage plaque, this unique Kitsilano oasis has been a beacon of food-growing best practice for almost 50 years. But while you can learn all about composting, vegetable gardening and sustainable urban agriculture from the super-friendly volunteers here, it's also the ideal spot to slow down and smell the roses—along with all the other flowers.

We've seen vibrantly blooming fuchsias, hollyhocks, ranunculus, red-slippers and dozens more on our visits. But don't expect a manicured botanical garden. Instead, it's a rustic idyll of higgledy-piggledy pathways winding between pocket-sized plots and raised beds. Adopt a snail's pace and you'll find plenty of delightful details—quirky artworks included (check out the goat on the cob shed roof).

You'll soon realize that silencing your phone increases the mental health benefits of coming here while also helping you tune into the abundant birdlife that's constantly popping by. On our most recent visit, we spotted several white-crowned sparrows and a couple of courting robins. Insects also thrive in the garden; look out for multiple Mason bee houses dotted around the site.

If your heart rate has also slowed to a snail's pace while you've been noodling around here, maybe it's time to consider starting (or restarting) your own garden. There's plenty of inspiration, of course, and everyone you meet here will be happy to offer practical advice—however green your thumb might be.

While you're in the area, save time to explore this end of the adjoining Arbutus Greenway. The former railtrack is now a popular walking and cycling route flanked by multiple gardens and allotment plots.

Nearby

- Old Hastings Mill Store Museum (p. 31)
- Kitsilano Showboat (p. 25)
- Heritage Harbour (p. 23)

COLBOURNE HOUSE

M&H

8743 SW Marine Drive, Vancouver

This rare example of a working-class home preserved for posterity is like a walk-in time capsule of yesteryear Vancouver. Rescued from demolition by intrepid volunteers—the City gave them a 60-year lease in 1994—the team has since worked tirelessly to restore the property to its 1930s heyday, when railway man Henry Colbourne and his family lived here.

Open on Wednesday mornings (excluding the final Wednesday of the month) and at other times by appointment, you'll be treated to a guided tour of a cozy little home brimming with intriguing features: a kitchen range that also heated the upper floor, a keepsake-studded living room with a Victrola record player, and a dining room table topped with fine china ready for a special occasion.

Upstairs—via steps that house a secret cupboard—are three small bedrooms suffused with nostalgia. On our visit, we spotted items that brought our own grandparents to mind, from Bakelite hairbrushes to colourful tobacco tins. The kids' bedrooms are filled with vintage toys, storybooks, scout badges and more.

Don't miss the downstairs backroom, a treasure trove of bygone items from butter makers to roller skates to pop bottles. And before you leave, ask your guide about the building that used to be next door—the childhood home of legendary Vancouver musician Dal Richards—then consider volunteering here with the friendly folks who are keeping this unique slice of local history so vibrantly alive.

The society that runs the house also operates several popular events throughout the year, including a summertime Treats, Treasures & Music happening that feels like a friendly garden party—complete with vendor stands and delicious goodies.

Nearby:

- Freecouvering Along the Fraser Foreshore Trail (p. 17)
- Mountain View Cemetery (p. 30)

CONTEMPORARY ART GALLERY

A&E

555 Nelson Street, Vancouver

Tucked between the entertainment district and historic Yaletown, the Contemporary Art Gallery (CAG) serves up a splash of colour and culture at the base of a condo tower on Nelson Street.

Admission is always free at the CAG, which is the longest-standing independent public gallery in Vancouver dedicated to contemporary art. It hosts exhibitions that rotate twice a year along with artist's talks, panel discussions, workshops, performances and special events. There is a small gift shop with art books and exhibition catalogues, an alcove with art for sale and two main gallery rooms.

In the Alvin Balkind Gallery to the right of the entrance, we enjoyed the meticulous sculptures of Douglas Watt's *Mayor of the Village* with model prop-like pieces, textures and textiles.

In the B.C. Binning Gallery, vast vertical canvases scale the height of the room, which is laid out like a maze for Ser Serpas's *rent.* The large-scale paintings contain sets of mirroring images made by imprinting one canvas onto another while still wet.

The CAG also curates an outdoor exhibit along the facade, and offsite at Yaletown–Roundhouse Station. There, we encountered Rafik Greiss's *Public Image*, an installation of photographs and videos reflecting on the complexities of movement and time.

The CAG regularly hosts free events and curatorial tours. One Saturday each month, a guest host is invited to lead walkthroughs of current exhibitions, offering their insights and response to the works on view. Visitors are also invited to email the gallery if they are interested in participating in family programs the gallery occasionally offers on and off site.

Nearby

- CPR Engine 374 (p. 12)
- BC Entertainment Hall of Fame StarWalk (p. 4)
- Vancouver Public Library Central Branch (p. 56)

CPR ENGINE 374

M&H

GFK

181 Roundhouse Mews, Vancouver

Vancouver has a poor track record (pun intended) for preserving its past. But at this cedar-beamed Yaletown pavilion, you'll meet perhaps the city's most famous historic artifact. Engine 374 is the locomotive that pulled the first transcontinental passenger train into Vancouver in 1887. This is your big chance to climb aboard, channel your inner train driver and give the bell a hearty ring.

But that's not all you can do at this small, family-friendly museum. The chatty volunteers are a font of knowledge about the grand old steam locomotive in their care. They'll tell you that it last ran in 1945 and was corroding at Kits Beach until the early 1980s when locals rallied to save it—their names are etched into the pavilion's brick-paved floor.

Four decades later, visitors still love communing with the immaculate engine and perusing the photos that include shots of the train's first arrival and images of long-gone Vancouver stations. There are also rail spikes, conductor hats and a gleaming 1950s CP Rail check-in counter you can step behind for some time-travelling selfies.

The original Stanley Park miniature locomotive is also displayed here, complete with smiling photos of kids riding it back in the day. You'll also be smiling if you visit during mid-May's Victoria Day weekend. On that Sunday, Engine 374 is typically pulled outside, and its 1887 Vancouver arrival party is emulated with free cake and live music.

While you're here, step outside and peruse the old turntable facility that's now a popular alfresco gathering place. Built in 1888, it displays some cool images of Yaletown's gritty railyard heyday.

Nearby

- Contemporary Art Gallery (p. 11)
- Vancouver Public Library Central Branch (p. 56)
- Freecouvering Around Yaletown (p. 60)

DEELEY EXHIBITION & MOTORCYLE MUSEUM

M&H

1875 Boundary Road, Vancouver

Canada's oldest Harley Davidson dealership isn't just for buyers; it's home to the country's largest privately owned collection of vintage motorcycles, and everyone is invited to check it out.

The Deeley family has been selling Harleys in Vancouver for over 100 years, starting out as a bicycle shop in 1914. The Deeley Exhibition & Motorcycle Museum displays a curated selection of over 55 brands—from Honda and Nimbus to Triumph, BMW and Suzuki (including the 1975 Suzuki RES Rotary, once named one of the ten worst motorcycles ever). With more than 250 bikes in the collection, the museum showroom, as spacious as it is, can't display them all at once, so themed exhibits rotate regularly. A donation of $5.00 is requested but not required.

One cruiser that caught our eye was the wooden Reitwagen, considered to be the first true motorcycle—and yes, it's made of wood. Before Daimler crafted it in 1885, motorcycles designs were based on steam engines. From rare vintage rides such as the 1917 Model F (the first model to use electric lights) to the 1963 Honda Super Cub (the most-produced motor vehicle in history), you'll learn something new while you admire the craftsmanship and mechanics of these two-wheeled machines.

You won't be able to miss the centrepiece of the collection, which rotates on a giant diamond-studded turntable: two Panzer replicas, including the Captain America of *Easy Rider* fame.

Before you leave, strike a pose in a sidecar, the one spot in the museum where you can climb aboard a steel steed and imagine the wind in your hair on the open road.

Nearby

- Slidey Slides Park (p. 37)
- Il Centro Italian Cultural Centre (p. 24)

EAST VAN VODVILLE CINEMA

A&E

**Fourth window from the alley,
1601 Venables Street, Vancouver**

Tucked away in East Vancouver, steps from busy Commercial Drive, you'll find the highly entertaining East Van Vodville Cinema. When we first visited, you really had to search along the sidewalk between boarded-up windows. Now, there's an awning welcoming you to the mini-theatre and inviting you to stay a little while longer while sheltering from any impending rain.

The window, smaller than a movie poster, is bordered by little light bulbs; the marquee is always updated to accurately reflect what's showing on the screen inside. Squint through the window, feeling like Gulliver in Lilliput, to see a 1:55 scale model of Vancouver's Pantages Theatre. At the time it was demolished in 2011, this red brick building on East Hastings Street was the oldest surviving vaudeville theatre in Canada. A sign next to the cinema details some of this history.

The Pantages's interior has been replicated in exquisite detail—you can even spot Statler and Waldorf (of Muppets fame) in the front-right balcony watching whatever short film is showing. The cinema has hosted a film festival and often presents themed programming in Technicolor or black and white.

The theatre is housed in the Vancouver Hack Space. If you happen to be there on a Tuesday afternoon at 4:30, visit their free open house to check out tools ranging from sewing machines to drill presses to 3D printers.

Before you leave, cross the street to the Slice of Life Gallery. Admission is a $5.00 donation, exhibitions rotate every few weeks and, best of all, there is a vintage pinball gallery where you can play as much as you like for an hourly rate.

Nearby

- Regional Assemby of Text's Letter Writing Club (p. 36)
- Il Centro Italian Cultural Centre (p. 24)

EMILY CARR UNIVERSITY GALLERIES

A&E

520 East 1st Avenue, Vancouver

World-renowned Emily Carr University of Art & Design (ECUAD) relocated from Granville Island to its striking new campus at False Creek Flats (South Flatz) in 2017, infusing the once-industrial area with creativity and colour.

Murals, plazas and the 2,000-square-foot Red Petal pavilion (housing a coffee shop) transform the exterior into an inviting gathering place for visitors, students and curious passersby alike. Inside, you'll find a number of free galleries that are open to the public.

The Libby Leshgold Gallery, right off the plaza along Great Northern Way, presents a rotation of exhibitions featuring established and emerging artists, with a focus on international dialogue in art and design. We caught *vertigo of swallows in my ear* by Hong-Kai Wang, which combined sound works with imagery and text.

Make your way down the stairs, past grand windows displaying an excellent view of the North Shore Mountains and the Skytrain whizzing by and pause to admire some of the Indigenous carvings on the doors to the Reliance Theatre. Continue down the halslway, past classrooms and studios on the lower level, to the Michael O'Brian Exhibition Commons. This is where the ECUAD community presents its work to the public, programmed by a rotating committee of students, faculty and staff. We enjoyed the mixed media approach also taken in this gallery, with photography, sound and video loops on two Commodore 64 units.

Outside and around the corner in the Wilson Arts Plaza, Urban Screen features moving image works blending campus life with culture and creativity for all passersby to enjoy.

Nearby

- Vancouver City Hall (p. 54)
- Spruce Harbour Marina History Walk (p. 39)
- Regional Assemby of Text's Letter Writing Club (p. 36)

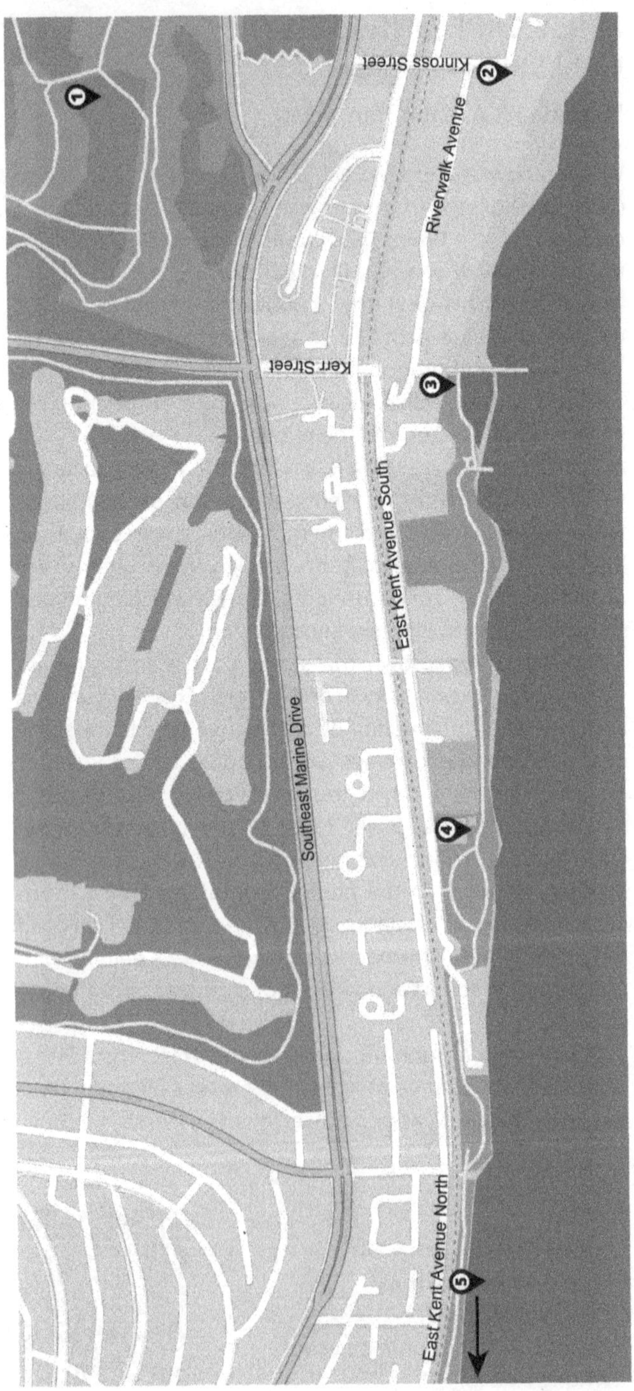
Kinross Street
Riverwalk Avenue
Kerr Street
East Kent Avenue South
Southeast Marine Drive
East Kent Avenue North

FREECOUVERING . . . ALONG THE FRASER FORESHORE TRAIL

Life in Metro Vancouver is shaped by the ocean, mountains and forests. The mighty Fraser River plays a defining role from **Fort Langley (p. 82)** and **New Westminster (p. 102)** to south Vancouver's River District, which borders the Fraser Foreshore Trail. This planned waterfront community has been gradually constructed on the sites of old sawmills and has more ambitious plans for the future.

Begin up on the hill in the 38-hectare **Everett Crowley Park (1)**, where you'll encounter a pond, creek and beautiful forest. Vancouver's fifth largest park, this verdant woodland bears not the slightest reminder that it was the site of a city landfill from 1944 to 1967.

From Everett Crowley Park, cross SE Marine Drive to start your riverside journey at **Kinross South Park (2)**, which features an epic playground with a waterslide tower, in-ground trampolines, sandbox with diggers, swings and plenty of places to climb and bounce. If you can pull the kids (and yourself) away from the fun here, walk or cycle towards the water and meet up with the Fraser Foreshore Trail, which you'll join at about its halfway mark. The trail starts almost 7 kilometres to the east in Burnaby.

Head west until you meet up with the **Kerr Street Pier (3)**. Enjoy the sights and sounds of the working river, from tugboats and barges to passing wildlife. You might spot an otter playing on a log boom or a great blue heron wading in the mud flats. There is a smaller playground and wooden public art sculpture as you continue east to **Riverfront Park (4)**, which offers basketball courts, a picnic area and athletic fields.

From there, follow the waterfront trail as it winds past wildflowers nestled under a lush, breezy canopy until you reach the final pier of the circuit at **Gladstone Riverside Park Pier (5)**. From this lookout along the north arm of the Fraser River, you can catch a beautiful sunset or lounge on one of the sun chairs by the pier as you read a book from the Little Free Library.

Nearby

- Colbourne House (p. 10)

FREECOUVERING . . . AROUND GASTOWN

In the neighbourhood where our modern-day city began, a slow wander around Gastown is all about discovering richly evocative reminders of the not-too-distant past. To whet your time-travelling appetite, start inside the grand, neoclassical **Waterfront Station (1)**.

Built by the Canadian Pacific Railway (CPR) in 1914, the last mainline train left here in 1979. It's now a bustling transit hub, linking SkyTrain, SeaBus and West Coast Express services. Glance at the easily missed painted panels near

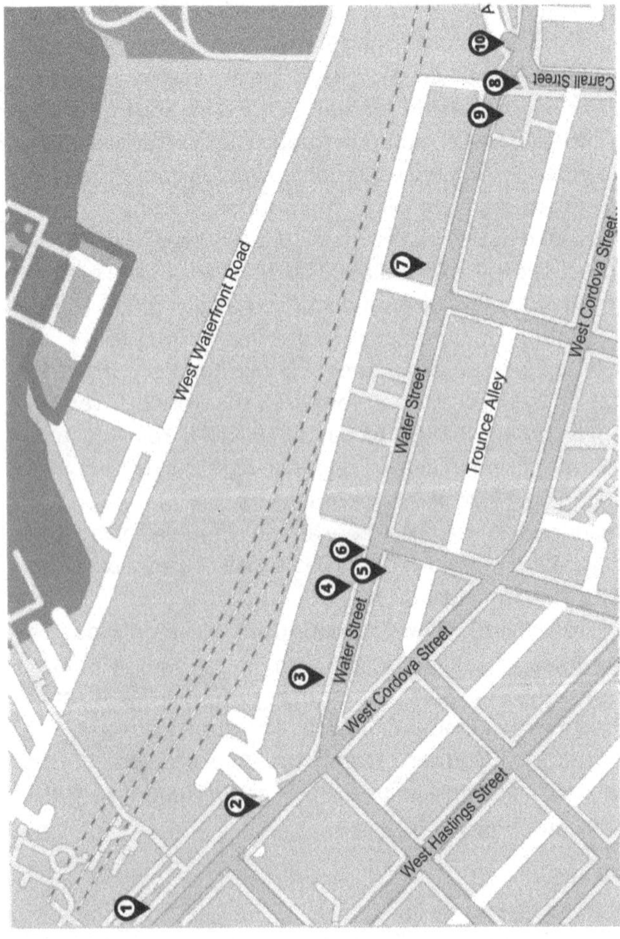

the ceiling, then head along the corridor to the left of the Rogue Kitchen & Wetbar restaurant.

Exiting via the station's side door, drink in the panoramic harbour views to your left before heading to the station's front facade on West Cordova Street. Here you'll find the ***Angel of Victory*** **(2)**, a moving memorial to CPR employees killed during the two world wars.

Orient yourself toward the nearby Steamworks Brewing, then hang a left along brick-paved Water Street. Gastown's main thoroughfare is lined with finely detailed heritage buildings—including the stone faces on the **Greenshields Building (3)** at No. 345. A few steps along, **Hudson House (4)** was built in 1895 as a Hudson's Bay Company warehouse. It was gutted by fire in 1972.

But the Great Fire of 1886 had a far more devastating impact on what was then a fledgling city, destroying up to 1,000 buildings. Across the street at **No. 302 (5)**, a plaque explains how the hotel that once stood here was the fire's only Gastown survivor. Not surprisingly, brick and stone replaced wood as the construction materials of choice.

Across the street, selfie-snapping crowds persistently gather around the **Steam Clock (6)**, a 1977-built postcard landmark with a steam whistle that sounds every 15 minutes (plus a tooting symphony on the hour). The mechanism itself is electrical.

Most of Gastown's handsome heritage buildings now house restaurants or boutiques. A few steps along Water Street brings you to arguably the most iconic. You don't have to buy anything to enjoy the gallery-like footwear temple otherwise known as **Fluevog Shoes (7)**, where the tables are topped with toe-hugging artworks.

Continue along Water Street until you reach **Maple Tree Square (8)**. The Victorian Italianate **Byrnes Block (9)** on your right is reputed to be the oldest Vancouver building still in its original location. It's opposite the former **Hotel Europe (10)**, an ornate rounded flatiron that has appeared in several movies and countless Gastown-themed artworks.

Nearby

- Freecouvering Around Chinatown (p. 6)
- Waterfront Photo Exhibit (p. 57)
- Port of Vancouver Discovery Centre (p. 34)

FREECOUVERING . . . AROUND GRANVILLE ISLAND

Before hitting Granville Island's cornucopia of cool stores, allow yourself to slow down and fully explore the picturesque peninsula (yes, it's not actually an island). Start underneath Anderson Street's red neon **Entry Sign (1)**, then turn right onto the boardwalk alongside the pond—scanning the water for springtime goslings and ducklings.

Continue past the playground until you reach the False Creek Racing Canoe Club's boat-packed shed. The faded **Ghost Sign (2)** on the adjoining building proclaims "SAWS Spear and Jackson Ltd." This is your introduction to Granville Island's gritty industrial past, when dozens of well-oiled workshops and small factories operated here.

Stay on the boardwalk—with Alder Bay on your right—until you reach **Ron Basford Park (3)**. Climb its zigzagging

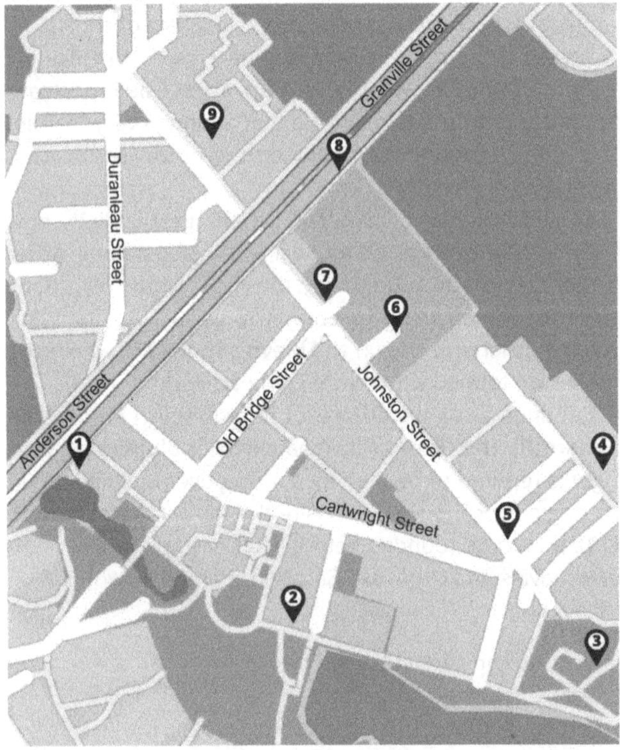

pathway to the grassy, picnic-friendly summit to enjoy some lofty panoramic views over the water and boat-bobbling marina. There's also a towering manmade eagle nest platform here, so be sure to check for chicks before you continue.

Back on the boardwalk, saunter around the tip of the island to find a colourful row of handsome **Houseboats (4)**. The steps alongside lead up to some rusting industrial heritage artifacts, including a hulking **Yellow Crane (5)** on rails. Pass underneath the crane and turn right onto Johnston Street towards a still-working reminder of Granville Island's tough-as-nails backstory.

Heidelberg Materials (6) is a busy cement plant where the 21-metre-high silos have been brilliantly transformed into a huge artwork: six gigantic humanoid characters spray-painted by Brazilian artists OSGEMEOS. Snap some photos, then continue along Johnston. On your right, you'll find the longhouse-style **Ocean Artworks Pavilion (7)** where—especially in summer—you might see expert Indigenous artists at work on their latest creations.

A few steps on and you'll find a boardwalk ramp on your right. Follow this to a shaded courtyard—home to an eclectic array of smaller outdoor artworks—then follow the boardwalk a little further until you find yourself right underneath the hulking **Granville Bridge (8)**. Look up and you'll spot hundreds of nesting cormorants using the historic ironwork span as their inner city home.

A few steps more and you'll reach the **Public Market (9)**, Granville Island's most popular visitor destination. If you need them, there are some good washrooms on the corner of the building here. Otherwise, head inside to browse the artisan stalls, deli vendors and piled-high fruit stands. There's also a food court here and some of the counters offer reduced-price meals at the end of the day.

Nearby

- Spruce Harbour Marina History Walk (p. 39)
- Vancouver Academy of Music (p. 52)
- Vancouver Archives (p. 53)

FAIRMONT HOTEL VANCOUVER MUSEUM

M&H

900 West Georgia Street, Vancouver

You might have already admired the Fairmont Hotel Vancouver, known as the Castle in the City, with its distinctive copper roof, dormers and gargoyles. But you can get up close to the hotel's history by visiting the small museum tucked away in its basement, where intimate artifacts from this storied landmark are on public display.

This building is the third to bear the name. The Canadian Pacific Railway built the first Hotel Vancouver in 1888 to attract weary travellers. In 1916, it was replaced with a larger and grander Italianate building located a block away (at the corner of Georgia and Howe Streets). Once considered one of the great hotels of the British Empire, it was demolished in 1949. You can find photos of this version of the hotel in the exhibit.

The current château-esque structure is one of Canada's grand railway hotels, and it was the tallest building in the city for decades after it opened in 1939. Take the stairs or elevator down one floor from the main lobby (at street level) to find display cases filled with photographs of celebrity guests ranging from King George VI to Zsa Zsa Gabor and George Carlin. You'll also find newspaper clippings, posters for a show in the Panorama Roof Ballroom, teacups and blueprints. Each item tells a story, offering a glimpse into the life of a city landmark. The vintage menus are a staggering throwback for any foodie, from a time when a prime rib roast dinner would set you back $1.55.

This iconic hotel's charm is distilled into artifacts that capture not only the glamour of the building itself but the pulse of Vancouver's social history. The hotel offers free history tours every Saturday at 2:00 pm. Stop by the concierge desk by 1:00 pm to secure your spot.

Nearby

- Vancouver Law Courts (p. 55)
- Pendulum Gallery (p. 33)
- Christ Church Cathedral (p. 8)

HERITAGE HARBOUR

M&H

1905 Ogden Avenue, Vancouver

The Vancouver Maritime Museum is well worth its admission price. But to keep your budget as ship-shape as possible, consider exploring their excellent Heritage Harbour area for free. Located on the nearby shoreline, it's a floating dock studded with colourful vintage boats—each with a plaque outlining its salty backstory.

You'll come face-to-face with vessels including retired lifeboat *Odin*, 1930s sailboat *Moonbeam*, Oregon fishing boat *Molly Sparks* and *Ern*, a wooden cutter built in 1956. Keen to learn how boats like these are constructed and restored? Drop by on Saturdays, when the friendly folks from Oarlock & Sail Wooden Boat Club work on projects in and around the dock's floating, shingle-sided shed.

Closer to the museum building, you'll find an eclectic array of additional alfresco exhibits. These include the *Ben Franklin*, a six-person submersible built in the 1960s for extended oceanographic study. There's also the boiler and paddlewheel shaft from Vancouver's most famous shipwreck, the SS *Beaver*, which sank off Stanley Park in 1888.

Speaking of wrecks, we also love the mysterious stone column resting on the grass here. In 1872, it was being transported from BC to adorn the exterior of the San Francisco Mint when its vessel sank. The 40-tonne column plunged into the sea and wasn't located for almost a century. In 1987, it was hoisted up and positioned outside the museum, where it's since become a popular perch for local crows.

> **Freecouver Tip** On the first Sunday of each month, the museum hosts its popular pay-what-you-can admission event.

Nearby

- Vancouver Archives (p. 53)
- Vancouver Academy of Music (p. 52)
- City Farmer Demonstration Garden (p. 9)

IL CENTRO ITALIAN CULTURAL CENTRE

M&H

A&E

3075 Slocan Street, Vancouver

As soon as you spot the flowering camellias, trickling water feature and Botticelli-like statues, you'll feel as if the charms of old Italy aren't too far away. Which is quite an achievement considering that Vancouver's Italian Cultural Centre occupies a 1970s concrete complex most tenants would find hard to warm up. Take your time, though, and you'll find several hot reasons to visit.

Start in the Il Museo room, which in recent years has curated an ever-changing roster of contemporary art exhibitions showcasing ceramics, paintings, tapestries and more. Near its entrance, don't miss the plaster sculptures of two monks tucked away in a cabinet. These were created by Italian Canadian artist Charles Marega, famous for fashioning the leonine landmarks you'll see on the **Lions Gate Bridge Walk** **(p. 26)**.

There's also a traditional Sicilian cart that's teeming with colourful carvings and brightly painted panels. Primarily used for transporting vegetables to market, these trundling folk-art wagons are extravagantly decorated and redeployed for saint's-day processions. Walk across the piazza outside to find a fully bedecked example—horse mannequin included—in its own glass display case.

Also in its own piazza display case, you'll find a stately and surprisingly large Venetian gondola. Originally transported to Vancouver for Expo '86 and donated to Il Centro shortly afterward, it's reputedly the only authentic example in North America.

Il Centro hosts regular events from film screenings to cooking classes here and also operates a popular restaurant—don't miss their happy hour deals, a delightful taste of *la dolce vita*.

Nearby

- Deeley Exhibition & Motorcyle Museum (p. 13)
- East Van Vodville Cinema (p. 14)

KITSILANO SHOWBOAT

A&E

GFK

2300 Cornwall Avenue, Vancouver

Typically operating from Wednesday to Sunday between mid-June and mid-August, this live entertainment legend near Kitsilano Beach is closing in on its 100th anniversary. Which, in an ever-changing place like Vancouver, is an astonishing achievement. But despite its longevity, this alfresco venue never rests on its laurels—and it's become a summertime staple for legions of in-the-know locals.

On languid summer evenings—with the sun setting to your left, the ocean glittering in English Bay and the mountains looming like a lofty chorus on the North Shore—it's hard to imagine a better place to be in the city. Snag a bleacher-style seat (sunhats, sunscreen and snacks recommended), switch off your phone and wait for the show to unfold on the blue-painted, paddle-steamer-themed stage.

A richly diverse roster of dozens of different performers hits the Showboat stage every season. That can range from rock bands to dance troupes, from kilted bagpipers to large orchestras, from jazz ensembles to flamenco strutters—and just about every other type of entertainment you can imagine. International cultures are always well represented; shows typically start at 7:00 pm.

Check this season's schedule to see what's coming up. And keep your calendar open for extra special performance days, including Canada Day, National Indigenous Peoples Day and more.

Freecouver Tip There's a kaleidoscopic array of free festivals throughout our region every year, ranging from arts events to live music to community showcases. Visit our website for a detailed list.

Nearby

- City Farmer Demonstration Garden (p. 9)
- Old Hastings Mill Store Museum (p. 31)

LIONS GATE BRIDGE WALK

G&N M&H A&E

Stanley Park Drive at Pipeline Road

A cheap thrill and the best skyline views of downtown Vancouver and the Stanley Park Seawall await when you head out for a stroll on the iconic Lions Gate Bridge. Built between 1937 and 1938 thanks to the Guinness family (of beer fame), who also developed West Vancouver's British Properties, it was officially opened by King George VI and Queen Elizabeth during a royal visit in 1939.

Starting from Pipeline Road at Stanley Park Drive (where the #19 bus will let you off before the roundabout), you can walk the length of the causeway through the forest, leading up to the bridge. Where the span meets the park on the south end, you'll be greeted by stone statues of lions designed by sculptor Charles Marega. The bridge, however, takes its name from the lion-shaped peaks that form part of the North Shore Mountains. Behind each lion is a plaque dedicated to various milestones and ceremonies over the last 90 years at this National Historic Site.

The path, separated from the three lanes of vehicle traffic by a curb and the suspension cables, widens into a roomy viewing platform at the base of each tower, a great place to stop for a photo. The deck might bump and shake a bit when two transit buses pass each other, adding to the excitement (or, in some cases, fear) of being 60 metres above Burrard Inlet's First Narrows.

Once you get to the north side, stop to admire the final views of the city, then follow the walkway as it dips below and under the bridge, bringing you back to the other side for your return trip. On the west side, you'll get an aerial view of the Capilano River and Ambleside Beach. Looking ahead, see if you can spot the Prospect Point lookout, where the Canadian, Vancouver and often navy flags wave.

Nearby:

- Stanley Park Attractions (p. 40–44)
- Freecouvering Around the West End (p. 58)

MARINE BUILDING

M&H

A&E

355 Burrard Street, Vancouver

When you visit Vancouver's beloved Art Deco skyscraper, be sure to pause outside. Completed in 1930 and briefly the tallest building in the British Empire, its exterior is adorned with plaster and brass biplanes, zeppelins and streamlined locomotives alongside stylized fish, turtles and octopuses—Jazz Age transportation innovations jostling for attention with vibrant sea creatures.

This extravagant detailing wasn't cheap, and the developer went bankrupt before the building even opened. But it's just a sample of what you'll find inside. Turn to the entrance—a grand archway of waving kelp and historic ships—and push through the revolving doors. In the lobby, you'll likely release several involuntary gasps as you try to drink it all in.

Like tiptoeing into an illuminated jewel box, the high-ceilinged interior is a shimmering spectacle of stained glass, glossy marble and richly elaborate detailing. Slow down and savour every inch. You'll spot a zodiac-themed floor, lofty sconces shaped like ships' prows and a large clock with ocean creatures in place of numbers (it was half-past seahorse on our visit).

Don't miss the seaweed-patterned elevator doors, which open onto dazzling interiors. Or the terracotta panels of Viking boats and incongruously grinning whales. Then duck into a decommissioned phone booth and pick up one of the old receivers to hear stories of 1920s Vancouver and the challenges involved in creating this cherished building. Now a protected heritage property, the Marine Building has found fame in film and television. In recent times, it has stood in for the Baxter Building in two Fantastic Four movies and for The Daily Planet in TV's *Smallville*.

Nearby

- Waterfront Photo Exhibit (p. 57)
- Port of Vancouver Discovery Centre (p. 34)
- Academie Duello's Swordplay Museum (p. 2)

FREECOUVERING . . . AROUND MOUNT PLEASANT

Start your Mount Pleasant experience with a smile at **Dude Chilling Park (1)**. This corner of Guelph Park was renamed by citizens inspired by the *Reclining Figure* statue by Michael Dennis. Next, head east on East 8th Avenue. This leafy residential street follows part of the path of Brewery Creek, named in honour of local 19th-century brewmasters, that used to flow

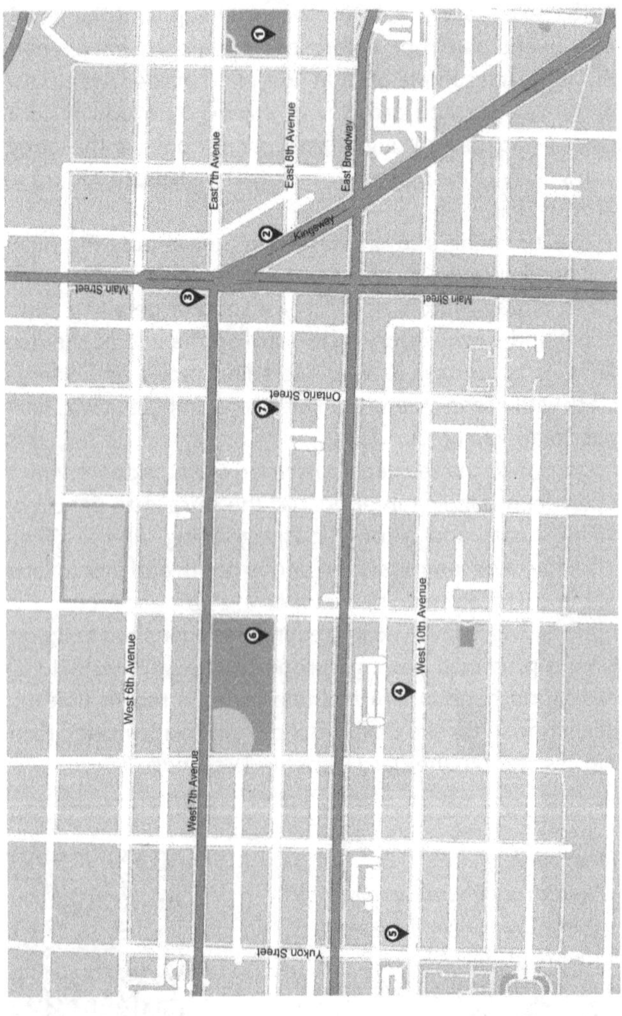

along the Mount Pleasant slope down to False Creek. Stop at the corner of **East 8th Avenue and Kingsway (2)**, where a four-sided marker provides details of this historic waterway.

Turn right on Kingsway for one block north to 7th Avenue, where it flows into Main Street. Cross both streets at the light and look down on the other side to spot some **Sidewalk Stamps (3)** shaped like streetcars. These are a tribute to the interurban streetcar system that once connected Vancouver with Burnaby, New Westminster and the Fraser Valley.

Head south on Main Street, which is back up the hill, and turn right on 10th Avenue where, in the 100 block, you can admire a row of beautifully preserved and brightly painted heritage houses, one of which is **Fred Welsh House (4)** at No. 144, a small Victorian-style home built in 1905 for a local grocer. The whole row of houses along West 10th between Manitoba and Columbia Streets was purchased and restored by the Davis family in the 1970s and 1980s; in their honour, locals call this the Davis Block.

Continue walking along 10th until you reach the corner of Yukon Street, where you'll spot a **Granite Marker (5)** with a small round sign. Installed in 1991, it tells the story of Dad's Cookies, a local franchise that began a block away (on Broadway) in 1930 and is now part of Nabisco Brands.

Turn right on Yukon Street and head across Broadway to 8th Avenue. Turn right again and you'll come to **Jonathan Rogers Park (6)**, where downtown Vancouver and the North Shore Mountains are laid out before you. In spring, this is a great spot for admiring cherry blossoms. But the main attraction here is courtesy of the Vancouver Mural Festival—you'll find vibrant murals on almost every building and down every alley until you reach the **Anza Club (7)** at the corner of 8th Avenue and Ontario Street, which also has a bright mural along its facade. The building was constructed in 1914 and acquired by the Australia New Zealand Association in 1969. Today, it's an event venue.

Nearby

- Quarry Gardens (p. 35)
- Vancouver City Hall (p. 54)
- Regional Assemby of Text's Letter Writing Club (p. 36)

MOUNTAIN VIEW CEMETERY

G&N

5455 Fraser Street, Vancouver

M&H

It may not be for everyone, but visiting a cemetery offers a unique outing among landscaped gardens, where each monument tells a story from the past. Founded in 1886, Mountain View, located in Vancouver's Riley Park–Little Mountain neighbourhood, is as old as the city itself. For those drawn to heritage and reflection, it's a stroll that reveals layers of the lives and times that shaped Vancouver.

Notable gravesites include Seraphim Joe Fortes (1863–1922), Vancouver's first lifeguard, who taught children to swim, saved 100 lives and was named Citizen of the Century by the Vancouver Historical Society; track and field record-breaker Harry Jerome (1940–1982); J. S. Matthews (1878–1970), an early historian and first archivist of the **Vancouver Archives (p. 53)**; and Sarah Anne McLagan (1855–1924), the first female publisher of a daily newspaper in Canada. Their graves lie alongside 14 former Vancouver mayors and generations of citizens. The City offers self-guided walking maps and a burial index available online so you can plot your course.

There are monuments to significant and tragic events in the City's past, including the sinking of the steamship *Princess Sophia*, railway crashes, the Rogers Pass Avalanche, and a streetcar disaster at Lakeview Station. In the springtime, trees bloom throughout the cemetery, and the Vancouver Cherry Blossom Festival hosts (paid) walks.

Visitors are asked to be respectful of the setting, the gravestones and mourners. This is for a quiet walk only, and not for cycling or picnicking.

Looking for more information? As part of the Royal BC Museum, the BC Archives maintains an online database of death certificates issued between 1872 and 2004.

Nearby:

- Quarry Gardens (p. 35)
- Colbourne House (p. 10)

OLD HASTINGS MILL STORE MUSEUM

M&H

1575 Alma Street, Vancouver

This building near Jericho Beach was constructed in 1868 and is still standing today, although it's about 10 kilometres from where it was originally built at the north foot of Dunlevy Street near Gastown.

By 1929, the Hastings Sawmill was closed, and its buildings were slated for demolition. Community groups rallied to save the Hastings Mill Store and Post Office, and in the summer of 1930, it was moved by boat along Burrard Inlet to its current location.

Donations are appreciated but not required for entry, which is through the post office section. It's packed with artifacts that give a glimpse of the early urban life of the city, which was incorporated in 1886. In a pram by the entranceway, we picked up a laminated ring-bound flip book that serves as a self-guided walking tour.

A lamp is not just a lamp in this museum. That's legendary lifeguard Joe Fortes' oil lamp. A chair isn't just any chair, it survived the Great Fire of 1886. That picture frame? It's made from wood salvaged from the SS *Beaver*, the Hudson's Bay steamship wrecked at Prospect Point in 1888. Those gloves? They were worn by Mayor McGeer at the opening of the new **Vancouver City Hall (p. 54)** in 1936. That rubber lacrosse ball carved from a 19th-century tractor tire? It was donated to the museum by Squamish Chief August Jack Khatsahlano, after whom the Kitsilano neighbourhood was named. And you won't be able to miss the entire Hansom Cab in the corner, donated by blacksmith George Jones.

Throughout the space, every typewriter, photograph and hairpin has a Vancouverite and a story attached to it.

Nearby

- City Farmer Demonstration Garden (p. 9)
- UBC Attractions (p. 45–51)
- Kitsilano Showboat (p. 25)

PACIFIC SPIRIT REGIONAL PARK

G&N

4915 West 16th Avenue, Vancouver

Metro Vancouver bristles like a cone-covered hemlock with great green spaces to visit. But the full benefits of communing with nature only come from slowing down and actively engaging your senses. That's where forest bathing comes in. An outdoorsy mindfulness method originating in Japan, forest bathing is all about being as present as possible in nature. Some parks offer scheduled events for a fee, but you don't need a guide to give it a try.

On our regular visits to this magnificent 860-hectare park, we stroll the tree-shaded trails until the joggers dissolve away and silence descends like a weighted blanket.

When you reach a sweet spot like this, stop and close your eyes. Breathe deeply and slowly and listen to every sound—from raven croaks to falling leaves. When your heartbeat slows, open your eyes and gaze at the forest as if for the first time. Notice the canopy arching above, the sky filling the gaps like a stained-glass window.

Gradually scan your surroundings for uncurling ferns or tree stumps shaped like ruined castles. Don't miss smaller details such as mushrooms, mossy carapaces and tiny residents—we recently spotted a slug that seemed to return our gaze when we leaned in.

You can search online for lots of additional forest bathing exercises. But the trick is to give yourself the time and permission to reconnect with nature while regrounding yourself—something we all need to do whenever we can.

Freecouver Tip Metro Vancouver Regional Parks host dozens of nature-hugging programs throughout the year—and many of them are free.

Nearby

- BC Golf Museum (p. 5)
- UBC Attractions (p. 45–51)
- Southlands Heritage Farm (p. 38)

PENDULUM GALLERY

A&E

885 West Georgia Street, Vancouver

Office buildings, with their blank white walls and unforgiving fluorescent lighting, aren't where you'd expect to find insightful, thought-provoking art. At RBC Place, however, the lobby is teeming with life beyond the echo of footsteps on polished stone floors.

When you enter from the street, across from the Vancouver Art Gallery, you'll find the aptly named Pendulum Gallery under a swinging metal arm reaching down seven stories from the glass atrium ceiling, swinging until it aligns at one end of its arc with an angled, stationary plinth. This public art piece, *Broken Column (Pendulum)* by Alan Storey is an attraction in its own right.

In this dramatic setting, the gallery is positioned between a cafe, a seating area, a grand piano and big, bright windows facing Hornby Street where it meets West Georgia.

This public cultural facility is focused on visual arts and includes a performance and exhibition space. Throughout the year, you might come across a fashion or architecture exhibit, historical photos or a showcase of underrepresented artists and arts communities from the region.

The exhibitions switch over about 12 times a year. During our visit, the gallery was showcasing works as part of the city's annual Capture Photography Festival, Western Canada's largest lens-based art festival.

Freecouver Tip Vancouver's sparkling array of public art is perfect for planning your own free artsy days out. From monumental installations to sidewalk mosaics to hidden gem statues, you can find out exactly where everything is via the City of Vancouver's online Public Art Registry.

Nearby

- Fairmont Hotel Vancouver Museum (p. 22)
- Vancouver Law Courts (p. 55)
- Christ Church Cathedral (p. 8)

PORT OF VANCOUVER DISCOVERY CENTRE

M&H

GFK

100 The Pointe, 999 Canada Place, Vancouver

Along downtown Vancouver's waterfront, under the iconic sails of Canada Place, you can watch seaplanes take off and land, and cruise ships come and go while you learn more about Canada's busiest port in the Port of Vancouver Discovery Centre.

Stroll down the Canadian Trail and spot names of cities from every province and territory enshrined in tile and coloured glass along the promenade. Before you reach the stairs for the (paid) FlyOver Canada attraction, you'll find the free exhibition, which is open daily from 8:00 am to 8:00 pm.

Discovery Centre displays cover the Salish Sea, local maritime history, shipbuilding and modern shipping. The space is one large room, with audio-visual commentary, interactive exhibits and artifacts that include a 19th-century nautical sextant and a model of Captain George Vancouver's HMS *Discovery*.

Wave your hand over the video display projected down from the ceiling to open captions and play vignettes. Hear from a blueberry farmer, tugboat captain or longshore worker—some of the many people who keep the port humming.

Outside, keep walking toward the north point for a great view of the port in action. The largest port in Canada, and the fourth largest in North America, what you can see is only a portion of the port's extensive network of terminals. Watch as colourful cargo containers get stacked and loaded onto ships like giant LEGO blocks. Time your visit for midday and you'll catch the *O Canada* horns, which echo across downtown Vancouver as they sound the first four notes of the national anthem.

Nearby

- Marine Building (p. 27)
- Waterfront Photo Exhibit (p. 57)
- Freecouvering Around Gastown (p. 18)

QUARRY GARDENS

G&N

Entrance at Cambie Street & West 33rd Avenue, Vancouver

Originally a basalt quarry site that closed in 1911, it took decades for the City of Vancouver to transform the 52-hectare Little Mountain area into Queen Elizabeth Park. And it wasn't until 1951 that Princess Elizabeth (two years from her own coronation; the park is named after her mother) planted the sapling that officially launched the park's grandest feature—its ornamental quarry gardens.

That sapling is now a strapping mature oak. And the Large Quarry Garden and Small Quarry Garden are now among Vancouver's greatest horticultural treasures, attracting legions of delighted visitors to their brilliantly vibrant flowerbeds. Depending on the season, the profusion of photogenic blooms here can include alliums, fritillaries, ranunculus, rhododendron and countless more.

On our visit, the waterfall that once cascaded under the larger garden's lofty bridge was being restored. It will feed into the ponds where you often see summertime turtles and dragonflies. Birds also thrive here—we've spotted wrens, towhees and deep-throated ravens croaking overhead. And we love the mini forest of giant rhubarb, where small dinosaurs might easily be hiding out.

Don't forget to explore the adjoining Small Quarry Garden as well. Accessed via a tree-lined pathway, it's similarly striped with expertly tended flowerbeds—there were huge swathes of sweet-smelling hyacinths on our visit. From here, you can ascend a short flight of steps to Vancouver's highest point, where you'll find breathtaking views over the mountain-framed city below.

If the budget allows, the nearby Bloedel Conservatory is excellent value. Entry was $9.50 at time of writing, with discounts for kids and seniors.

Nearby

- Mountain View Cemetery (p. 30)
- Vancouver City Hall (p. 54)
- Freecouvering Around Mount Pleasant (p. 28)

REGIONAL ASSEMBY OF TEXT'S LETTER WRITING CLUB

A&E

3934 Main Street, Vancouver

For two decades, the Regional Assembly of Text has taken a determinedly analogue approach to life. The friendly little stationery store is famous for stocking everything from perfect journals to pencil sets—alongside an unrivalled array of house-made greetings cards and quirky chap-books with titles such as *Mister Mitten* and *One Shrew Too Few*.

But in-the-know locals keen to escape from their smart-phones also love dropping by on the first Thursday of the month. That's when the store's early-evening Letter Writing Club takes over the space, providing a great opportunity to clack away on a vintage typewriter in a warm and chatty long-table setting.

It's a good idea to line up outside by 6:00 pm. There are two sittings, and you'll know by 7:00 pm if you're going to snag a seat in front of one of the Remingtons or Smith Coronas. Once you're in, grab some paper from the counter and you'll soon be hammering out that heartfelt love letter, frame-worthy list of life goals or multi-stanza ode to the Canucks you've been waiting to immortalize.

Throughout the evening, your hosts will be on-hand to instruct you in the ways of old-school tech—lots of par-ticipants have never touched a typewriter before. They'll also troubleshoot finicky issues from key jams to mangled ribbons. And if you need a break to rest your aching finger muscles, tea and cookies are generously provided.

While you're here, duck into the tiny lowercase reading room (yes, even the name is lowercased), located in a little side-nook. Its shelves house hundreds of carefully curated zines and self-published minibooks; there's even a small seat where you can sit and browse.

Nearby

- East Van Vodville Cinema (p. 14)
- Emily Carr University Galleries (p. 15)
- Freecouvering Around Mount Pleasant (p. 28)

SLIDEY SLIDES PARK

G&N | M&H
GFK | A&E

3311 East Hastings Street, Vancouver

Slidey Slides Park is the playground formerly known as Plateau Park in the area formerly known as Empire Stadium. Named by schoolchildren and set in a location where the Beatles and Elvis Presley once took to the stage, Slidey Slides offers swings and climbing surfaces on the site of an international drama that shook the sporting world.

Empire Stadium stood at the PNE site in Hastings Park until it was demolished in 1993. Its biggest sporting moment—the Miracle Mile at the 1954 Commonwealth Games—is commemorated by a statue at the north side of the track. Frozen in time forever are England's Roger Bannister and Australian John Landy, the first two men to break the four-minute-mile barrier. The statue depicts Landry glancing over his shoulder during the last 90 yards of their race, which Bannister went on to win.

The playground is located on the east side of the park between Playland's Wooden Roller Coaster and the former stadium's turf soccer fields. The actual slidey slides are built into the hillside between the plateau and the track area that encloses the fields. There's also a beach volleyball court, a parkour course, basketball and table tennis. The southeast corner is home to the Leeside Skate Park. This 7-metre-high, 49-metre-long abandoned tunnel is popular with skateboarders and BMXers.

In the northwest corner stands *Home+Away*, a functional art installation with 16 rows of seating rising like a pie-slice of the old stadium. Climbing to the top yields panoramic views of East Vancouver, Burnaby, Burrard Inlet and the North Shore Mountains. Instead of scoreboards and floodlights, there are swings creaking in the breeze, the roar of the stadium crowd now softened into children's laughter.

Nearby

- Deeley Exhibition & Motorcyle Museum (p. 13)
- Burnaby Mountain Conservation Area (p. 95)

SOUTHLANDS HERITAGE FARM

G&N

GFK

3208 West 51st Avenue, Vancouver

Tucked into the rustic but wealthy Southlands neighbourhood—a semi-rural Vancouver enclave of large homes with adjoining stables from which horses peer inquisitively at passersby—this compact farm site is popular with local families. Many of them book ahead for the (paid) horse-riding experiences that have been enjoyed by junior visitors for decades.

But you don't have to saddle up to appreciate the farm's bucolic charms. Open to the public (donations are welcome), you can explore its winding willow-fenced pathways and snap photos of the flowers, veggie plots and active beehives. Keep your eyes peeled for information panels on nature and sustainable farming, as well as the wandering wildfowl that noodle in and around the pond.

You'll soon find yourself at the farm's gabled stable building, where you can meet resident equines Sprite, Foxy, Groot and more—this is your chance to practice your whinnying skills. When you exit the barn, you'll also find a fenced enclosure of beady-eyed Muscovy ducks and plump heritage chickens with handsome feather patterns.

For a critter-based finale, head into the goat pen to socialize with some friendly hairballs, including energetic summer newborns. And before you leave, visit the farm stand for eggs and own-grown produce. There's also an aromatic shed filled with free manure if you have room in your backpack. Time to spare? Explore the wider Southlands neighbourhood on foot—while staying alert for passing horse traffic.

A few steps away, the lovely Southlands Nursery is a delightful, oasis-like garden centre jam-packed with amazingly vibrant plants—and everything you need to grow them yourself.

Nearby

- BC Golf Museum (p. 5)
- UBC Attractions (p. 45–51)
- Pacific Spirit Regional Park (p. 32)

SPRUCE HARBOUR MARINA HISTORY WALK

G&N
M&H

1015 Ironwork Passage, Vancouver

If you're walking, riding or strolling between Leg-in-Boot Square and Granville Island along the seawall in False Creek, you can get a surprise history and ecology lesson near the entrance to the Spruce Harbour Marina.

While the marina docks are gated and private, for members only, the marina, along with the Greater Vancouver Floating Home Co-operative, has installed ten displays along the Island Park Walk where it splits and runs parallel to the Ironwork Passage (the main seawall path).

Each display panel features information about what you're observing in the area. Identify waterfowl by referring to the large colour photographs and descriptions of migratory birds, read about how the co-operative's collection of "tiny homes on the water" functions, and make note of the ever-changing downtown skyline across the water. Today you'll see yachts and glistening towers where historic photographs show sooty railyards, lumber mills and log booms.

Compare your view with the displays of vintage photos sourced from the **Vancouver Archives (p. 53)** that show what the view looked like 100 years ago. Line up your shots to match the perspectives of the black and white W.J. Moore panoramas to make your own "Then and Now" set.

This stop is also an excellent vantage point for watching little boats ferry foot passengers to destinations along the shore, as well as spotting harbour seals and watching dragon boat clubs practice on the waterway.

If you'd like to learn more, scan the QR code to download a history of False Creek that includes a map of the many creeks that lie buried beneath surrounding streets.

Nearby:

- Emily Carr University Galleries (p. 15)
- Freecouvering Around Granville Island (p. 20)

STANLEY PARK GARDENS

G&N

Stanley Park, Vancouver

The cultivated gardens of Stanley Park offer idyllic spots for picnics, photographs and a glimpse into the city's history.

Rose Garden From Miranda Lambert and Beverly, Easy Going to Fiji Eleganza, Stanley Park Rose Garden boasts over 3,500 rose bushes that have been meticulously maintained for over a century. From July to September, seasonal blooms like towering dahlias complement the rose beds, as do cherry blossoms from March to May.

Shakespeare Garden A stone monument to the Bard stands in one of the park's most curiously fragrant spots: between the Rose Garden and the Vancouver Police Mounted Unit stables. Fanning out from the brick column are forty species of trees mentioned in Shakespeare's poetry and plays. The first tree was planted in 1916, marking the 300th anniversary of his death. Over the years, some have been lost to the elements, and others have grown so tall that the plaques bearing their references now sit well above eye level, so you may have to look up to spot them.

Ted and Mary Greig Rhododendron Garden Between Lost Lagoon and the Pitch and Putt, there is a bountiful collection of over 4,500 hybrid rhododendrons and azaleas planted in the 1960s that bloom between March and September.

Rocks The City of Vancouver's first public garden was famous for its rocks. The Stanley Park Rock Garden opened in 1910 and became a popular attraction. Over the years, it fell into neglect, disappearing into the surrounding forest after the Second World War. It remained hidden until a powerful windstorm in 2006 toppled trees and revealed parts of the long-lost garden, sparking efforts to restore it.

Nearby

- Stanley Park Attractions (p. 40–44)
- Lions Gate Bridge Walk (p. 26)
- Freecouvering Around the West End (p. 58)

STANLEY PARK INDIGENOUS ART

A&E | G&N | M&H

Stanley Park, Vancouver

The most popular tourist destination in BC, the first Stanley Park totem poles were acquired from First Nations based on Vancouver Island and the Central Coast and installed in the 1920s. Though the park sits on the traditional, unceded territory of the xʷməθkʷəy̓əm (Musqueam), Sḵwx̱wú7mesh (Squamish) and səlilwətaɬ (Tsleil-Waututh) Nations, it wasn't until 2008 that carvings by local nations were finally unveiled here.

Begin your visit from the downtown side of the Seawall. Pass beneath the first of three beautifully carved gateway arches by Musqueam artist Susan Point. This welcome portal leads you into a gravel plaza nestled between Brockton Point Fields, the forest, Coal Harbour and Burrard Inlet. It's a place layered with history, culture and connection.

There are nine other totems on site, each with signage that introduces the carver and the totem's features. One of the most recent poles to be added, the first from the Sḵwx̱wú7mesh (Squamish) Nation, was carved by Robert Yelton and installed in 2009 to honour his relative, Rose Cole Yelton, and all who once lived in Stanley Park. The pole is situated in front of the house site where the Cole family lived until 1935.

Don't miss the bronze *Shore to Shore*, unveiled in 2015, tucked behind the totem viewing area at the western tip of the parking lot. Depicting "Portuguese Joe" Silvey and his Coast Salish wives, Khaltinaht and Kwatleematt, it was the first sculpture in a Vancouver park to include historical female figures. If you'd like a deeper understanding, Squamish and Sechelt-owned Talaysay Tours offers engaging guided experiences that explore the park's living history, culture, and native plants for a fee. (See talaysay.com).

Nearby

- Stanley Park Attractions (p. 40–44)
- Lions Gate Bridge Walk (p. 26)
- Freecouvering Around the West End (p. 58)

STANLEY PARK NATURE HOUSE

G&N

GFK

712 Lost Lagoon Path, Vancouver

Before hitting the lovely tree-shaded trails and exploring Stanley Park's amazing wild side for yourself, brush up on its temperate rainforest flora and fauna at this friendly and inviting interpretative centre. Tucked along the Lost Lagoon shoreline, you'll find engaging exhibits on everything from skulls to scat, fungus to feathers.

We especially love the tooth-and-claw taxidermy on display here—including ducks, owls, a recently acquired bald eagle and a fierce red-tailed hawk that looks more than ready to land on your head and pluck out your eyeballs. In contrast, the stuffed beaver seems far more approachable, and you can even (gently) stroke its soft fur.

We also love the bird nests exhibits—including teardrop-shaped bushtit dwellings—and a small cabinet that illustrates the eye-popping size and colour differences between the eggs of Canada geese, American goldfinches and more. There's also a huge slice of a 360-year-old Douglas fir that fell during Vancouver's infamous 2006 storm, alongside 10,000 other park trees.

Quiz the knowledgeable volunteers about that fateful day and ask them any other nature questions you can think of. They can also point you to some great park trails. Before you leave, check out their spotting scope located just outside the building. Trained on Lost Lagoon, you might see herons, turtles and perhaps even a beaver gliding through the water—don't try to stroke it, though.

Speaking of herons, Stanley Park is home to a celebrated heronry just a short walk away from the Nature House. Every spring, dozens of hopeful avian parents turn up in the trees here to build nests, lay eggs and (fingers crossed) raise a gangly baby or two. You can gaze up and watch them in action, but look out for falling fecal matter!

Nearby

- Stanley Park Attractions (p. 40–44)
- Lions Gate Bridge Walk (p. 26)
- Freecouvering Around the West End (p. 58)

STANLEY PARK STATUES AND MONUMENTS

A&E | G&N | M&H

Stanley Park, Vancouver

Scotland's Robert Burns enjoys one of the best views in the city, standing on a hill above the Stanley Park Rowing Club. The tribute to the Ploughman Poet was the first full statue installed in Vancouver, in 1928. The first likeness, however, was David Oppenheimer (the city's second mayor), whose bust was installed at the park's western entrance, off Beach Avenue, in 1911. The Queen Victoria Memorial Drinking Fountain, just to the east of Burns, was unveiled in 1906.

By Third Beach, you'll find a memorial cairn dedicated to Pauline Johnson (Tekahionwake), a celebrated writer and poet of Haudenosaunee and English descent whose words still echo through the park—she first gave Lost Lagoon its name.

Pause to reflect at the Japanese Canadian War Memorial located between the aquarium and Lumberman's Arch. The granite column rises from a quiet garden of cherry blossom trees planted in 1932.

The 6-metre-tall *Chief of the Undersea World*, by celebrated Haida artist Bill Reid, is in the middle of a fountain outside the Vancouver Aquarium. Perched on a granite boulder in Burrard Inlet is Elek Imredy's bronze *Girl in a Wetsuit,* often assumed to be a mermaid. In a small plaza nearby, you'll find the colourful *Empress of Japan* figurehead, a fiberglass reproduction that commemorates a ship that crossed the Pacific between 1891-1922. At Hallelujah Point sits a tribute to local track star Harry Jerome, who set seven world records. The Harding Memorial at Malkin Bowl marks the visit of the first American president to speak in Vancouver, in July 1923, just a week before passing away unexpectedly in Seattle.

Nearby

- Stanley Park Attractions (p. 40–44)
- Lions Gate Bridge Walk (p. 26)
- Freecouvering Around the West End (p. 58)

STANLEY PARK VANCOUVER NAVAL MUSEUM

M&H

GFK

Stanley Park, Vancouver

The very first order of business at the City of Vancouver's first council meeting in 1886 was to petition the British government to lease their military reserve for use as a park. To this day, the Royal Canadian Navy maintains its position on Stanley Park's Deadman's Island.

The museum is packed with collections that include a who's who of prominent Vancouverites who served, photographs and medals, ships' crests, medical devices and musical instruments, uniforms and maps, hand-painted miniature replicas of significant ships and aircraft carriers, and a comprehensive section dedicated to WRENS (Women's Royal Canadian Naval Service).

The only admission cost is a signature in the guestbook, but you will normally need to book in advance. On the occasional sunny day, they'll put a sign out by the big blue gate along the Seawall listing times for public guided tours.

Due to Department of National Defence security constraints at this working base, hours may be limited, or you might be turned away even with an appointment. If that happens, just connect with the museum and they'll happily book you in for another time.

While you're nearby, stroll along the Seawall to the Nine O'clock Gun, just past the **Harry Jerome statue (p. 43)**. In the 19th century, this muzzle-loaded naval cannon was used by the Department of Marine and Fisheries to signal the 6:00 pm close of Sunday fishing. Today, it's a time signal, fired nightly at 9:00 pm, although on occasion it's off by a minute or two. Plug your ears if you're there at 8:59 pm—a red light and alarm will warn you when it's about to BOOM!

Nearby

- Stanley Park Attractions (p. 40–44)
- Lions Gate Bridge Walk (p. 26)
- Freecouvering Around the West End (p. 58)

UBC BELKIN ART GALLERY

A&E

G&N

1825 Main Mall, Vancouver

The UBC campus is jam-packed with photo-friendly alfresco artworks just waiting to be discovered—so long as you have the time and energy to track them all down. But if the weather is unwelcoming or you just want to muse over some chin-stroking creativity in a gallery celebrated for its thoughtful, often challenging exhibits, the Belkin is the place for you.

Founded in 1948 as the UBC Fine Arts Gallery—Vancouver's first to focus entirely on contemporary works—the gallery moved to its current site in 1995, renaming itself after its Morris and Helen Belkin benefactors. The white-walled, high-ceiling space is famously tranquil and inviting, despite presenting what might be regarded as difficult works that typically address weighty societal issues (past themes have included time, power and wildfires).

Exhibitions change quarterly and you might see bold paintings, peculiar video presentations or eye-popping multimedia installations fashioned from Perspex, neon, obsidian, balsa wood and more. The trick is to slow down, open your mind and tune in to the creations in a kind of mindful, forest-bathing approach to art.

Before you leave, ask the friendly front desker for a free map of UBC's outdoor art. It pinpoints 24 diverse on-campus works well worth tracking down. You'll find amazing murals, hidden sculptures, Indigenous carvings and—our personal favourite—Rodney Graham's *Millennial Time Machine*, a glass pavilion housing a full-sized landau carriage that's been converted into a camera obscura.

The Belkin regularly hosts free guided art walks on the campus. You'll find the details of any upcoming walks listed on their website.

Nearby

- BC Golf Museum (p. 5)
- Pacific Spirit Regional Park (p. 32)
- Southlands Heritage Farm (p. 38)
- UBC Attractions (p. 45–51)

UBC CHUNG | LIND GALLERY

A&E

M&H

1961 East Mall, Vancouver

Head up to the second level of UBC's Irving K. Barber Learning Centre, and you'll find this excellent little museum space. Showcasing two richly evocative collections that bring to life three overlapping areas of Canadian history, spend at least an hour immersing yourself in the artifacts, photos and stories here, including the bonus drawers beneath many cabinets.

The Wallace B. Chung and Madeline H. Chung Collection explores the lives of early Chinese immigrants in BC, from their dangerous work constructing Canada's railways to settlement and even prosperity in Vancouver and beyond, often in the face of rampant racism. Those harsh, sometimes fatal railway jobs contrast sharply with the Chung Collection's second focus.

The Canadian Pacific Railway Company promoted the ineffable glamour of passenger travel—from cross-country train adventures to international steamship odysseys—via famously alluring advertising posters. The gallery includes many top-notch examples of this colourful graphic art, showcasing everything from 128-day boat trips from New York to "delightful cruises to the West Indies."

You'll also find posters in the gallery's Phil Lind Klondike Gold Rush section, where 1930s' movies romanticized a frantic 19th-century mass-migration that ruined thousands of nugget-crazed men. Peruse the photos of fur-swaddled prospectors, Dawson City saloon drinkers and the women who travelled north to part greenhorns from their gold. Don't miss the tiny model cabin with its 3D projection of a lone prospector and his dog moving around inside.

You'll find the same eye-catching technology deployed near the museum's entrance, where a model of the *Empress of Asia* steamship floats on a digital ocean.

Nearby

- BC Golf Museum (p. 5)
- Pacific Spirit Regional Park (p. 32)
- Southlands Heritage Farm (p. 38)
- UBC Attractions (p. 45–51)

UBC FARM

G&N

GFK

3461 Ross Drive, Vancouver

The city feels very far away when you're strolling the tractor-rutted trails around this bucolic, 24-hectare farm—sometimes with the kind of pungent aromas only a country-dweller could love. But as you explore the patchwork of tree-framed fields, large greenhouses and experimental growing areas, you'll appreciate just how much work is going on at the Centre for Sustainable Food Systems' main research and teaching facility.

Many visitors come for the June to November farmers' market. In addition to selling produce, the farm was a founding member of the BC Ecoseed Coop, which sells certified organic vegetable and flower seeds on site and via an online catalogue.

While there's a cornucopia of additional onsite events throughout the year, we recommend dropping by on quieter days to experience everything from the fascinating Indigenous Health Research and Teaching Garden to the tranquil Agroforestry Trail that leads you through the adjoining woodland.

On our visit, we were especially intrigued by the truffière orchard, where the BC cultivation of Mediterranean black winter truffles is being actively researched. It's just across from a carefully manicured heritage apple orchard where dozens of unusual varieties and multiple growing methods are being carefully studied.

We also spotted a towering and unruly-looking hedgerow alongside a freshly ploughed field. A once-common agricultural sight, these rich bird and insect habitats hugely increase a farm's biodiversity. Speaking of insects, we were delighted to find a row of bright-painted beehives that were bristling with buzz-tastic action—a perfect finale to any farm visit.

Nearby

- BC Golf Museum (p. 5)
- Pacific Spirit Regional Park (p. 32)
- Southlands Heritage Farm (p. 38)
- UBC Attractions (p. 45–51)

UBC INDIGENOUS OUTDOOR ART

M&H | A&E | G&N

University of British Columbia Campus, Vancouver

UBC is located on the ancestral and unceded territory of the xʷməθkʷəy̓əm (Musqueam) people. So it's fitting that its Point Grey campus is studded with remarkable Indigenous art. Many of these are on the map linked to the QR code, but we also recommend picking up *qeqən: A Walking Tour of Musqueam House Posts at UBC*, a free booklet available from the **Belkin Art Gallery (p. 45).**

On your campus exploration, you'll find the dramatic, 10-metre-high *Musqueam Post* near the UBC Bookstore. Encircled by a two-headed serpent and situated on a terraced water feature, this spectacular carving by Brent Sparrow Jr. tells the ancient origin story of the Musqueam name—its accompanying information panel explains more.

A far darker history is painfully and painstakingly depicted on James Hart's *Reconciliation Pole* on Main Mall. This deeply moving carving encourages reflection on Canada's residential school period, when thousands of children were taken from their families to be assimilated into settler society, a process that saw their rich cultural identities supressed and their history deliberately erased.

There are many additional amazing works to track down (we love Thomas Cannell's carving, *Thunder*, for example). But save time for the Museum of Anthropology. This excellent attraction isn't free (although half-price admission is offered on Thursday evenings), but you don't have to pay to follow the trail that leads around the back of the building. Here, you'll find a replica Haida village, several large carvings and an ocean lookout where eagles swoop past.

When you return to the front entrance, check out the artworks in and around the Welcome Plaza. You'll find brilliant creations here by Susan Point and Joe Becker.

Nearby

- BC Golf Museum (p. 5)
- Pacific Spirit Regional Park (p. 32)
- Southlands Heritage Farm (p. 38)
- UBC Attractions (p. 45–51)

UBC PACIFIC MUSEUM OF EARTH

G&N

M&H

GFK

6339 Stores Road, Vancouver

There's a cornucopia of kid-friendly exhibits at this sparkling UBC attraction. And by sparkling, we mean multiple cabinets filled with glittering minerals and gemstones—from opals to diamonds and more. But this museum doesn't just showcase dazzling treasures in their natural form. In fact, there's so much more to see that repeat visits are essential.

Fossil fans will find plenty to peruse, from a mammoth tooth to a large dinosaur thighbone you can actually touch. A star attraction is "George," the wall-mounted skeleton of a duck-billed Lambeosaurus excavated in Alberta in 1913. He's arguably the museum's most photographed exhibit. But he's definitely not the only display worth pointing your lens at.

Switch to night-shoot mode and enter the darkened room where gold nuggets and jewellery are showcased—alongside a globe-shaped animated projection of the Earth illustrating its key processes. Next, return to the main room to find (and touch) the Acasta Gneiss exhibit. This unassuming black-grey stone from the Northwest Territories claims to be the world's oldest rock at 4.03 billion years and counting.

Despite its admission-free philosophy (donations are welcome), there are many more exhibits to discover at this museum. Check out the explanatory displays on volcanoes and wildfires. Learn about how oceans work. And then step in front of a green screen to broadcast the weather live on TV—we "entertained" everyone with our dramatically over-the-top Vancouver rainfall forecast.

Before you leave, check out the exhibits in adjoining buildings, then trace the Earth's story over billions of years at the outdoor Wheaton *Walk Through Time* display.

Nearby

- BC Golf Museum (p. 5)
- Pacific Spirit Regional Park (p. 32)
- Southlands Heritage Farm (p. 38)
- UBC Attractions (p. 45–51)

UBC ROY BARNETT RECITAL HALL

A&E

6361 Memorial Road, Vancouver

In-the-know music lovers regularly check UBC School of Music's online calendar to see what's coming up at this intimate, 255-seat recital hall situated on a tree-lined side street in the heart of the Point Grey campus. There are typically several daytime and evening performances here every week, and a gratifyingly large proportion of them are completely free to attend.

The surprisingly diverse array of shows—everything from classical to contemporary to world music—can include student recitals, ensemble performances or appearances by faculty or visiting musicians. On our visit, we caught a brilliantly energetic performance by the UBC Korean Drumming Club, complete with costumed participants and intriguingly unfamiliar percussion instruments.

This particular performance was staged in the sunny alfresco plaza immediately outside the theatre. If you're sitting in the theatre at the appointed time and nothing seems to be happening on stage, head outside and you'll likely find the show!

Wondering who the recital hall is named after? When music-loving UBC alumnus Roy Barnett retired from a long and distinguished business career, he decided to finally learn to play the piano—at the age of 72. Inspired by the process as well as his enduring love for music, he donated $2 million to renovate the venue, helping to support musicians, performance and education for years to come.

Freecouver Tip Every summer, CBC's downtown Vancouver headquarters stages Musical Nooners, an outdoor series of diverse, toe-tapping and totally free lunchtime concerts.

Nearby

- BC Golf Museum (p. 5)
- Pacific Spirit Regional Park (p. 32)
- Southlands Heritage Farm (p. 38)
- UBC Attractions (p. 45–51)

UBC TRIUMF PUBLIC TOUR

M&H

4004 Wesbrook Mall, Vancouver

Arguably Vancouver's most unusual guided tour, this is your big chance for an up-close encounter with the world's largest cyclotron. And if you're not sure what a cyclotron is (strangely, it has nothing to do with bicycles), that's the perfect reason to book your timeslot, meet the whip-smart researcher leading your visit and go behind the scenes at this unique UBC site.

A collaboration between multiple universities, TRIUMF is one of Canada's two main particle accelerator facilities. Using a different technology than Switzerland's CERN hadron collider, its six-bladed, 18-metre-diameter cyclotron swirls hydrogen ions to three-quarters the speed of light. The resulting protons are then used for crucial study, research and medical applications.

Don't worry, you don't need to be a physics major to enjoy this tour. Walking through the halls, you'll spot sci-fi-looking experimental areas packed with huge magnets, cable-covered machinery and banks of winking servers. Along the way, you'll see a darkened computer-filled control room that operates 24-7 and a pastel-coloured scale model that helps explain how the cyclotron actually works.

That model is located on top of the thick concrete carapace that covers the cyclotron—you'll be standing on this during your tour. If the cyclotron is operating during your visit, this is also where your guide will treat you to some entertaining tricks. We don't want to spoil the surprise, but let's just say your magnetic personality will come shining through.

If you're inspired to learn more about the wonderful world of physics, consider TRIUMF's public, all-ages Saturday morning lectures. These free drop-in events are staged here or at locations around the region.

Nearby

- BC Golf Museum (p. 5)
- Pacific Spirit Regional Park (p. 32)
- Southlands Heritage Farm (p. 38)
- UBC Attractions (p. 45–51)

VANCOUVER ACADEMY OF MUSIC

A&E

1270 Chestnut Street, Vancouver

GFK

Located in Vanier Park opposite the Museum of Vancouver (where we recommend pay-what-you-can admission on the first Sunday of every month), this musical education centre is a magnet for in-the-know performance fans. Dozens of public concerts are staged here throughout the year—and almost all of them are free. Peruse the VAM website to see what's coming up, then drop by and take a seat.

There are two main performance spaces here. The larger Koerner Recital Hall stages a surprisingly wide array of events that range from student concerts to junior symphony demonstrations, and from top-level masterclass performances to spine-tingling shows by elite VAM or visiting musicians. Composer-wise, you might catch anyone from Brahms to Vivaldi to Tchaikovsky—while also discovering works by artists you haven't heard of before.

One of the VAM's most popular programs is their Adult Learning Program, which offers private and group classes for late bloomers wanting to master a variety of instruments. These intrepid souls perform Soirée Concerts in the Koerner Recital Hall at regular intervals. Admission is free.

The Mary Olson Hall is a much smaller, more intimate space. Its main contribution to VAM's free-show roster is the monthly Strawberry & Tea student concerts, where younger artists perform pieces they have recently mastered. All levels of learning are showcased in these matinee events. On our visit, we were continually amazed by the talent and virtuosity on display from the dozen or so piano, violin, harp and flute performers who each performed one or two short pieces to enthusiastic applause.

Nearby

- Heritage Harbour (p. 23)
- Vancouver Archives (p. 53)
- Freecouvering Around Granville Island (p. 20)

VANCOUVER ARCHIVES

M&H

1150 Chestnut Street, Vancouver

This stop can be a real treat for any history buff. The City of Vancouver Archives are located in the Major Matthews Building in Kitsilano's Vanier Park, named after Major J.S. Matthews, Vancouver's foremost documentarian and collector, who was appointed the city's first archivist in 1933. When this bunker-like facility opened in 1972, it was the first in Canada built specifically to house a city archive. Previous locations for the holdings included various nooks and crannies in City Hall or the library.

The archives contain more than seven million images that document multiple aspects of Vancouver history and culture from the 1860s to today, along with thousands of maps, artifacts, city council minutes and more.

There is also a small gallery space where, on our visit, we enjoyed pieces from a guest exhibit, *Artists in the Archives*, by an **Emily Carr University class (p. 15).** While the Reading Room is primarily reserved for registered researchers, the public is welcome to pop in to inquire about an old house location, a photograph or a newspaper article.

> **Freecouver Tip** It may seem like we're giving you homework, but you can find an excellent souvenir of Vancouver when you search through the Vancouver Archives' online database. Sort your query to look for photos in the public domain only, meaning they are free of copyright or trademark. Search for a cool vintage aerial or panoramic image, save the file and print it out at home to make your own unique postcard or wall art.

Nearby

- Heritage Harbour (p. 23)
- Vancouver Academy of Music (p. 52)
- Freecouvering Around Granville Island (p. 20)

VANCOUVER CITY HALL

M&H

A&E

453 West 12th Avenue, Vancouver

Check in at the security desk and begin your self-guided tour of the Depression-era Art Deco monument that is Vancouver City Hall. Built between 1935 and 1936, there are plaques along the marble walls that commemorate councils from each of those years, plus other notable guests and milestones for the city. There are fine details and modernist influences in everything from the stairwell signs and elevator button panels to the building directory and brass mail slot.

Be sure to take a walk around the outside of the building, where you'll find a statue of Captain George Vancouver, the city's namesake, on the north side. Take in the panoramic views of the downtown skyline against the stunning backdrop of the North Shore Mountains from Helena Gutteridge Plaza. In 1937, Gutteridge became the first woman elected to Vancouver City Council.

Look up at the building, admire photo-op-worthy staircases, public art pieces, a Japanese garden and a bronze bust of former mayor G.G. McGeer. According to Heritage Vancouver, McGeer saw the construction of City Hall as a morale lift for Vancouverites and was confident that the new building would provide jobs and amplify the celebration of Vancouver's Golden Jubilee.

Visitors are welcome to admire the building's history and architecture on weekdays between 8:30 am and 5:00 pm. Check the schedule online to see when City Council is in session; you can sit in on the meetings from the third-floor viewing area with its brass sconces, high walls and veneered wall panels. Come for the architecture, stay for the high-stakes political drama—or routine municipal procedures.

Nearby

- Emily Carr University Galleries (p. 15)
- Quarry Gardens (p. 35)
- Freecouvering Around Mount Pleasant (p. 28)

VANCOUVER LAW COURTS

M&H

800 Smithe Street, Vancouver

You can't miss the huge glass-and-concrete courthouse complex (designed by Arthur Erickson) that stretches for two blocks south of downtown's Robson Square. But did you know that the public is encouraged to visit and experience Canada's multifaceted legal system in action here?

Comprising the Provincial Court, Supreme Court and Court of Appeal, we recommend encountering the latter two via the building's Nelson Street entrance. Inside its greenhouse-style atrium, you'll spot bronze busts of famous judges and a statue of Themis, goddess of justice. You can then peruse the blue computer screens listing the day's cases, start times and courtroom numbers.

If you don't have a specific case in mind, simply stroll the hallways between the courtrooms. The rule is that you can enter any courtroom where the exterior doors are wide open, take a seat inside and leave whenever you are ready. Cameras and recording devices are prohibited.

On our visit, one courtroom had officers and airport-style security outside. Heading in, we found a suspect behind bulletproof glass facing a judge who was listening intently to a defence barrister. This was a hearing to address a specific issue in a larger trial—for murder.

Keep in mind that even big cases like this are rarely as dramatic as their TV depictions. But the opportunity to bear witness to legal proceedings is a crucial feature of our civil society, and that's something all of us should experience at least once.

> **Freecouver Tip** Have your own ice skates? You can triple salchow for free all winter at Robson Square Ice Rink, located right beside the Law Courts.

Nearby

- Pendulum Gallery (p. 33)
- Fairmont Hotel Vancouver Museum (p. 22)
- Freecouvering Around Yaletown (p. 60)

VANCOUVER PUBLIC LIBRARY CENTRAL BRANCH

A&E
G&N
GFK

350 West Georgia Street, Vancouver

When architect Moshe Safdie designed Vancouver's new city centre library—the photogenic, Colosseum-like landmark opened in 1995—he envisioned a place for locals to convene and connect rather than just hunkering down in silence. Traditionalists rolled their eyes, but Safdie's vision was inspired, even though it took years for everything to finally fall into place.

Today, while stacks and study carrels dominate the Central Branch's curved interior, many visitors head straight to the ninth-level Phillips, Hager and North Garden. Part of Safdie's original plans, this checkerboard plein air plaza, Vancouver's first public rooftop garden, didn't open until 2018. But it's a great place to snag a sun-kissed seat among lofty blossom trees and fragrant flowerbeds.

Don't spend all your time eyeballing the elevated city views, though. Instead, head back inside and explore the bright and airy eighth floor. An even greater distillation of Safdie's gathering place philosophy, it's lined with gallery-quality artworks from the library's own collection, including a small photo exhibit profiling yesteryear operations at previous Central Branch incarnations.

This floor also offers loaner board games, theatre-room movie screenings and a performance space with bleacher-style seating (a cool marimba band was playing on our visit). VPL's online calendar lists lots of upcoming free events at this library—including monthly guided tours that explain its services and take you around Safdie's remarkable building. On our tour, we heard all about the reinvented Children's Library floor set to reopen after a major renovation. It promises a huge, multi-level reading tree that kids can hang out in and under.

Nearby

- CPR Engine 374 (p. 12)
- Contemporary Art Gallery (p. 11)
- Freecouvering Around Yaletown (p. 60)

WATERFRONT PHOTO EXHIBIT

M&H

Waterfront Centre Food Court,
200 Burrard Street, Vancouver

This under-the-radar photography display is a great way to see exactly what Vancouver looked like in the early days. Lining both sides of the subterranean walkway between Waterfront Centre Food Court and Canada Place, it comprises 21 large-format monochrome images from 1886 (when the city was incorporated) to the 1940s, when it was already a buzzing metropolis.

Near the start, you'll find two famous Vancouver scenes. In the first, a new City Hall has been erected—a tent with a hand-painted sign—just after the Great Fire of 1886 decimated the settlement. In the second—a few months later—locals in the rapidly recovering city are cheering the momentous arrival of the first transcontinental passenger train. The train is pulled by **CPR Engine 374 (p. 12)**, now proudly displayed in Yaletown.

The richly evocative photos that follow show just how quickly the city developed over the ensuing decades. Take your time as you peer into the past and you'll spot lots of amazing slice-of-life details. There's a butcher store bristling with cuts, carcasses and stony-faced staff (smiling for the camera was—quite literally—frowned upon at the time).

There's also a bustling downtown scene with busy pedestrians, rattling streetcars and a turreted former incarnation of the Hotel Vancouver. We particularly love the 1925 photo of a city-centre newsstand. Plastered with magazines, it has a small sign advertising snacks ("Cakes 5 cents" and "Sandwiches 10 cents") as well as a selection of "Light Reading for Winter Evenings."

Want to know more? The Vancouver Library has an enormous collection of photos that can be searched via the QR code below.

Nearby

- Marine Building (p. 27)
- Port of Vancouver Discovery Centre (p. 34)
- Freecouvering Around Gastown (p. 18)

FREECOUVERING . . . AROUND THE WEST END

Start your West End jaunt in the heart of Davie Village at **Jim Deva Plaza (1)**, named for a beloved 2SLGBTQIA+ and anti-censorship activist. Surrounded by rainbow crosswalks and banners, the plaza hosts markets, performances and community art displays. Make your way down the slope, through the quiet neighbourhood where you'll end up at **Sunset Beach Park (2)** along the Seawall. Spot public art pieces as you head northwest (away from the Burrard Bridge and toward the mountains), including the rusty whale rib, aka Bernar Venet's *217.5 Arc x 13,* and further up the path on the grassy hill, two giant rings that make up Dennis Oppenheim's *Engagement.*

Standing alone on the waterfront is the **Inukshuk (3)**. It was commissioned by the Northwest Territories for Expo 86 in Vancouver and later became the inspiration for the

Vancouver 2010 Olympics logo. English Bay Beach is now in sight but pop up to Alexandra Park across Beach Avenue for a look at the granite and bronze **Joe Fortes Drinking Fountain (4)**, named in honour of Vancouver's Citizen of the Century, a prominent figure in the early days of the West End and BC Black history. Cross back over to the sandy beach or continue along the avenue to the triangle of 1800 Davie Plaza and Morton Park, where you'll find the ***A-maze-ing Laughter Statues* (5)**. These 14 bronze figures by artist Yue Minjun bring smiles to the faces of visitors and locals alike and are a popular spot for photos.

Continue down Denman Street from Davie and spot the murals along your route as you angle up Comox Street, past Lord Roberts School, and hang a left on Nicola. On the corner of Nicola and Nelson is **Firehall No. 6 (6)**, the first purpose-built fire hall in North America for motorized trucks, built in 1907 and still serving today. Continue north on Nicola and you'll soon see grand old manors on the corner of Barclay Street. Behind them is **Barclay Heritage Square (7)**, an urban oasis with gardens and a dog park. Nearby, you'll see Roedde House Museum (admission by donation). Turn left onto Broughton Street, past Roedde House's gazebo, then make a quick right on Haro Street for the last climb of your journey. Shady trees will cover you on this quiet residential thoroughfare and bike route, just a block off bustling Robson Street. Bute Street is your destination, with a pedestrian plaza to the right, and the new **Bute Robson Plaza (8)** to your left. From this peak at Haro and Bute, you can see clear through downtown Vancouver all the way to Burrard Inlet and the North Shore.

Popular events in the area include the Vancouver Pride Parade and Festival (the largest of its kind in North America) and the free Lumiere Festival that lights up the neighbourhood in November. In the summer, the sounds of Jazz on the Porch (hosted by Roedde House) echo throughout the neighbourhood.

Nearby

- Stanley Park Attractions (p. 40-44)
- Lions Gate Bridge Walk (p. 26)

FREECOUVERING . . . AROUND YALETOWN

Start your Yaletown exploration at the **Roundhouse Community Centre (1)** near the intersection of Davie Street and Pacific Boulevard. The building's rear exterior courtyard features a preserved railroad turntable (built in 1888) that used to move and organize up to 20 locomotives. The vintage photo panels in the centre of the now pedestrianized turntable include yesteryear images of it in action.

For a more hands-on steam train experience, enter the adjoining **CPR Engine 374 (p. 12) (2).** The locomotive that pulled the first transcontinental passenger train into Van-

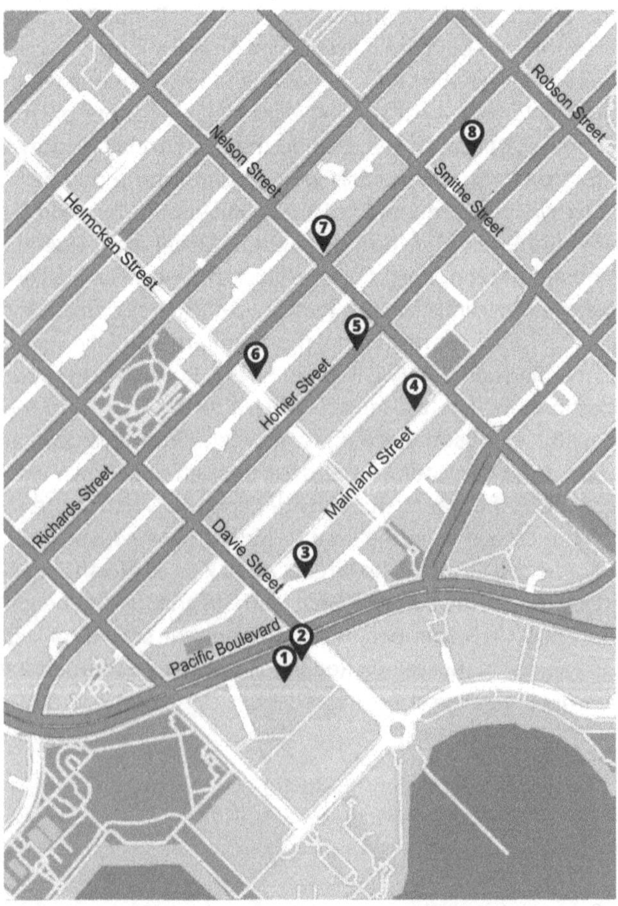

couver in 1887 is proudly displayed here, alongside some fascinating historic exhibits. Keep in mind that although latter-day Yaletown is one of the city's ritziest areas, it started life as a gritty rail yard and warehouse district.

You'll get a feel for that era as you walk up the incline of Davie and turn right along Mainland Street. Notice the elevated sidewalks on one side—about the height of a railway station platform—where goods trains used to trundle in and unload. A few steps along Mainland, take a seat in **Bill Curtis Square (3)**—there are often dozens of colourful umbrellas artfully strung overhead like lanterns here.

Continue along Mainland, glancing at the upper levels of the vintage warehouse buildings, most of them now cleverly converted into offices and loft apartments. Then cross to the other side of the street. Passing alongside a string of popular restaurants, you'll notice some chunky and unusual **Bench Seats (4)**. These were made from thick Douglas fir timbers reclaimed from some of the area's old warehouses.

Turn left along Nelson Street until you reach Homer, turning left again along this leafy thoroughfare. At 1014, glance at the **Stall Building (5)**, a handsome Art Deco structure that used to be occupied by General Motors. At the next intersection, turn right along Helmcken, where you'll soon spot five beautifully preserved **Heritage Houses (6)**. Built in 1907, these are the last of many workers' cottages built in the area.

Take the next right-hand turn along Richards Street. You'll soon spot the **Contemporary Art Gallery (p. 11) (7)** on your left. Head inside or continue along Richards to Smithe Street until you reach one of Vancouver's most striking and relatively new urban parks. Known as **Rainbow Park (8)**—as well as by its Indigenous name sθəqəlxenəm ts'exwts'áxwi7—it features a hugely popular playground (check out that towering tube slide!) plus a zigzagging steel walkway that bisects it from above.

Nearby

- CPR Engine 374 (p. 12)
- Vancouver Law Courts (p. 55)
- Vancouver Public Library Central Branch (p. 56)

Richmond & Delta

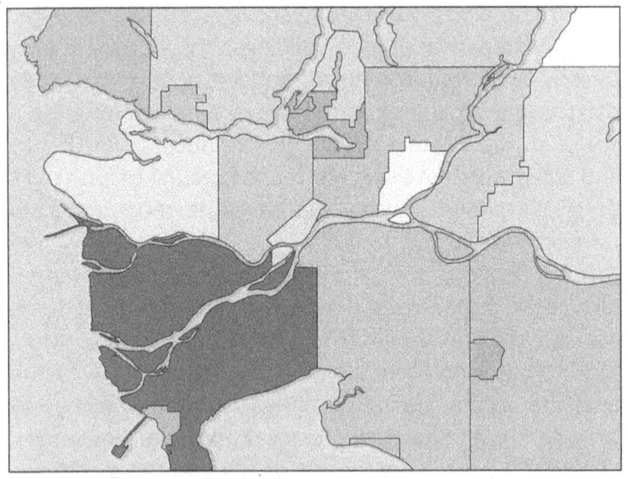

BRITANNIA SHIPYARDS NATIONAL HISTORIC SITE

M&H

GFK

5180 Westwater Drive, Richmond

A scenic shoreline stroll from the heart of Steveston Village, visiting Britannia Shipyards is like stepping back in time. A boardwalk hamlet of preserved sheds, net lofts and accommodations where fishing, canning and boatbuilding workers once toiled, this atmospheric 20-hectare site brings the past to life brilliantly.

At the Chinese Bunkhouse, you'll see how immigrant cannery workers were crammed into narrow, triple-decker beds. Audio recordings, a short movie and a recreated kitchen illuminate the gritty minutiae of daily existence. Nearby, a row of shingle-sided homes on stilts includes the far more palatial Manager's Cottage.

But Britannia's most moving exhibit is Murakami House, where a boatbuilding and fishing family thrived—until 1942, when the wartime government forced thousands of Japanese Canadians into internment camps. The home has been meticulously recreated with personal touches including a wooden *furo* bath and a family-tree bedspread.

A few steps away, Britannia's main building looms over the riverfront. Built as a cannery in 1889 and later transformed into a shipyard and boat repair facility, it's full of tools, workshops and old machinery—oily aromas included. In fact, it feels as though a grease-smeared worker of yesteryear might walk past at any moment.

Nearby, the Seine Net Loft focuses on BC's fishing heritage, with vintage signage, old engines and a fascinating pilot-wheel-making area. Before you leave, hit the Richmond Boat Builders shed where restoration projects take place. On our visit, a 1963 gillnetter was slowly returning to its pristine glory.

Nearby

- Steveston Tram (p. 73)
- Steveston Museum & Post Office (p. 72)
- Freecouvering Around Steveston (p. 74)

DOUGLAS J. HUBBARD DISCOVERY CENTRE

M&H

GFK

4450 Clarence Taylor Crescent, Delta

The Douglas J. Husband Discovery Centre is home to the Delta Museum & Archives, where admission is free and learning about geology, farming and local culture is fun and interactive.

The city, bordered by the Fraser River, Boundary Bay, Surrey and the Salish Sea, includes the communities of Ladner, Tsawwassen and North Delta. The museum shares Coast Salish history along with stories of settlers from Norway, Finland, Japan and beyond.

Learn how Delta became home to British Columbia's first cannery in 1871. Don't miss out on drawers and slots that say "Open Me" or "Take a Closer Look" as they'll reveal even more artifacts, including a piece of wood from the Bronze Age that was found in Burns Bog (North America's largest sphagnum peat bog).

We loved reading about Punjabi farmers and Japanese fishers and the legend of colourful characters like Pansy May who, some stories say, oversaw a Prohibition-era rum-running operation from her residence on the bluffs. Touchscreens allow you to swipe your hand across archive photos and modern-day snaps of the same scene to compare the views.

Younger visitors can pick up colouring sheets and scavenger hunt clues at the entrance. Stop by the post office display for a blank postcard on which you can draw a memorable item from the gallery to make your own souvenir.

Kids and adults alike will delight in interactive features like the waving of a special wand that moves a cursor around a video projection of local wildlife, or the water table that demonstrates how the Fraser River delta was formed over the course of 9,000 years.

Nearby

• Richmond Country Farms (p. 69)

INTERNATIONAL BUDDHIST TEMPLE

M&H

9160 Steveston Highway, Richmond

Respectful visitors are always welcome at this dazzling, traditional-style temple complex in southern Richmond. The trick is to slow down and give yourself plenty of time to explore every single detail. Keep in mind that photos are allowed in the exterior area—complete with water features, a deer-themed garden and more—but frowned upon inside, where sacred halls and active shrines operate.

In that outside area, you'll be greeted by a smiling, big-bellied Buddha statue and a plaque inviting you to "Always Maintain a Joyous Mind." That's not hard to achieve here as you stroll around the pond, spot statues of cranes and turtles, and glimpse multiple terracotta-tiled buildings waiting for you—there's a handy wall map here telling you exactly what each building is.

Next, head through the open gate into the inner complex. A feast for the senses, incense aromas abound as you discover the Gracious Hall. It houses a huge golden statue of Avalokitesvara Bodhisattva—symbol of infinite compassion—flanked by an array of richly detailed, highly expressive figures. Whether or not you are a follower, it's hard not to feel reverential here.

But that's not all. Continue exploring and you'll discover more shrines, ancient limestone formations, countless carved and painted features, and even a large reclining Buddha statue enjoying a beautifully beatific siesta. Inspired to learn more about Buddhism during your visit? There are several little bookshops dotted around the complex that specialize in educational tomes and more.

If you're keen to launch a wider-ranging religious exploration, consider visiting the more than 20 religious facilities that line No. 5 Road, Richmond's "Highway to Heaven."

Nearby

- Richmond Country Farms (p. 69)
- Paulik Neighbourhood Park (p. 68)
- London Farm (p. 67)

LARRY BERG FLIGHT PATH PARK

G&N

GFK

Russ Baker Way & Airport Road, Richmond

At Larry Berg Flight Path Park, one of Metro Vancouver's most unusual small parks, you'll be serenaded by the deafening roar of departing airplanes. But that's the point. This grassy, picnic-friendly greenspace is located just past the perimeter fence of Vancouver International Airport's (YVR's) busy south runway—and visitors of all ages love dropping by to have their conversations continually drowned out.

Named after a former CEO of the Vancouver International Airport Authority, there are some cool aviation-themed features to check out, including paths painted like runways and seats resembling paper airplanes. Kids also love climbing the huge, dome-shaped globe section that depicts destination distances from Vancouver—Addis Ababa seems to be the farthest at 13,311 kilometres.

Adults are not forgotten, though. We love the YVR factoids mounted on tailfin-shaped panels here. You'll learn that the airport opened in 1931, soon after Charles Lindbergh said Vancouver had "no fit field to land on." You'll also read that each new daily long-haul service adds 150 jobs to the airport. And you'll discover that 20 percent of all flights here are floatplanes or helicopters.

You can learn more about the huge variety of aircraft that use the airport from some additional information panels nearby. But since these were badly faded on our visit, we recommend simply sitting on a runway-facing seat and looking up. Within seconds, your eardrums will be vibrating as you scan the undercarriage of a departing plane that seems almost close enough to touch.

Keep in mind that this park is hugely popular during the springtime blossom season, attracting photo-snappers from around the region.

Nearby

- Richmond Cultural Centre (p. 70)
- Richmond Nature House (p. 71)

LONDON FARM

G&N

GFK

6511 Dyke Road, Richmond

Bordering the South Arm of the Fraser River, London Farm's verdant parkland grounds are accessible year-round; its charming historic home is open from May to September. Whatever time of year you visit, you'll be connecting with the pioneering London family that resided here from 1888 to the 1940s.

Weaving around the grounds' well-marked pathways, you'll find information panels showing exactly what it was like to live and work here. Several red-painted barns have also been handsomely restored with displays of vintage tools, photos of yesteryear and even a hulking old threshing machine that looks like it probably sliced a few fingers off back in the day.

Don't miss the delightful flower garden—often bursting with dahlias and roses in summer—before you head up the steps into the white-painted wooden farmhouse. Built in the late 1800s and expanded several times over the ensuing years, its antique-lined main floor includes a dining room and a large parlour, plus an additional room where afternoon teas are often served (book ahead for these).

You'll spot several photos of the former residents as you climb the creaking staircase to the second floor, where small bedrooms have been brought to life with children's toys, Sunday-best dresses and lots of nostalgic knick-knacks. Back on the main floor, save time to peruse the little gift shop area where they often sell delicious jams made from fruit grown on the property.

There are typically several free, kid-friendly special events held at London Farm every year, including an August Family Farm Day and a September Country Fest.

Nearby

- International Buddhist Temple (p. 65)
- Richmond Country Farms (p. 69)

PAULIK NEIGHBOURHOOD PARK

G&N

7620 Heather Street, Richmond

Located alongside an unassuming Richmond residential street, ducking between the towering conifers here is like a Narnia wardrobe trip to another realm. This 2.4-hectare neighbourhood park has all the standard paths and picnic tables, but it also houses a hidden gem regarded by many as a secret botanical garden.

Not that it's really a secret. Lovingly overseen by the friendly folks of the Richmond Garden Club, their skills and dedication have forged a green-thumbed utopia where sun-dappled pathways link busy beds bursting with flowering plant life. Depending on the season, that can mean anything from lilies to lupines, hellebores to hyacinths or huge bursts of floofy rhododendrons in vibrant hues.

Alongside a soundtrack of twittering birds and under the watchful gaze of resident rabbits, you'll also find countless whimsical garden sculptures and installations dotted between the foliage here—our favourite is the seahorse. We even found a kid-friendly butterfly area with large panels to help you identify the six local lepidopterans that might flit by at any moment.

You might also spot Garden Club members beavering away in the beds. They're happy to offer gardening tips, and they host both free and paid classes and workshops (richmondgardenclub.ca/events). They're not the only ones: Urban Bounty also has an office in this park, and they offer a roster of free gardening events around Richmond (urbanbounty.ca/events/workshop) that can include themes such as garden mindfullness or practical topics such as native plants and organic gardening methods. Be sure to reserve ahead as space is limited.

Nearby

- International Buddhist Temple (p. 65)
- Richmond Cultural Centre (p. 70)
- Richmond Nature House (p. 71)

RICHMOND COUNTRY FARMS

G&N

GFK

12900 Steveston Highway, Richmond

Typically open daily from mid-April to the end of the Halloween season, this massively popular farm-stand complex is much more than just a great place to peruse a huge variety of fresh produce. When we come here, we quickly explore the piled-high displays in and around the red barn, then stroll across to the large, white-fenced animal enclosures.

You don't have to be a kid to enjoy hanging out with the farm animals here. We love snapping photos of everything from the strutting turkeys to the snuffling, curly-haired pigs. There are also lots of keen-eyed goats that come over to greet you—in summer, you'll typically see several energetic little goaty youngsters gambolling around the paddock.

You'll also be serenaded by several breeds of cock-a-doodling chickens, some of them wandering outside the fences as if they own the place. Explore the bucolic grounds yourself and you'll spot some gracefully rusting vintage tractors—especially near the onsite winery, where well-priced bottles of chardonnay, cabernet franc and more are available.

Keep in mind that Richmond Country Farms also hosts two paid events during the year (summer's Sunflower Festival and fall's Pumpkin Patch). And note that the variety of fresh produce available here changes frequently as the seasons progress—we especially look forward to their sweet local strawberries and tasty own-grown Warba potatoes. Don't forget to add Richmond's famous annual blueberry crop to your treat list as well; they typically arrive here from early July onwards.

Nearby

- Douglas J. Hubbard Discovery Centre (p. 64)
- International Buddhist Temple (p. 65)
- London Farm (p. 67)

RICHMOND CULTURAL CENTRE

M&H

A&E

7700 Minoru Gate, Richmond

Start your visit at the Richmond Art Gallery (richmondartgallery.org). This double-roomed, white-walled space stages a diverse array of contemporary art shows throughout the year, featuring artists working in textiles, video, ceramics and more. Consider timing your visit for an exhibition opening; these free, friendly events feature tours, curator talks and light refreshments. The gallery also regularly hosts free or low-cost workshops where you can tap into your otherwise hidden creativity.

Located right next door, the smaller Richmond Museum (richmondmuseum.ca) presents one major exhibition per year, which typically changes in September. These cleverly curated shows often explore fascinating, sometimes unexpected aspects of the local community. Past exhibitions have focused on everything from esoteric private collections to the city's rich skateboarding heritage.

A few steps away, dive deeper into history at the City of Richmond Archives (richmond.ca/archives). An active research facility, visitors are invited to peruse its wall-mounted timeline of photos and videos tracing the city's development. You'll also find an engaging exhibit on Richmond's Japanese Canadian Harada family here—complete with highly evocative photos and artifacts from 1900 onwards.

Additional historic photos are usually displayed in the nearby Minoru Hall Gallery—there were some lively images of Richmond's old Brighouse Racetrack on our visit. If you have time, check out the building's second-level Rotunda Gallery, where additional art displays are often featured. You can also access the Rooftop Garden from here—a bee-friendly floral oasis where you can sit and contemplate your immersive Cultural Centre visit.

Nearby

- Paulik Neighbourhood Park (p. 68)
- Larry Berg Flight Path Park (p. 66)
- Richmond Nature House (p. 71)

RICHMOND NATURE HOUSE

G&N

GFK

11851 Westminster Highway, Richmond

This warm and inviting facility, located at the entrance to Richmond Nature Park, is a great place to introduce kids to nature. Start in the activity corner where they'll have fun identifying local critters on a painted tree display and perusing several real-life critters in glass tanks, everything from Pacific tree frogs to Northwestern Gartersnakes and more.

Nearby, you'll find excellent interpretive displays on bees, pullout drawers with local plant samples and easy-to-use microscopes for scrutinizing your chosen insect slides. We also love the menagerie of top-notch taxidermy on display, with tooth-and-claw skunks, coyotes, barn owls and more, all waiting to be photographed.

The friendly staffers here are always happy to answer questions about local flora and fauna; there are also regular events and activities to consider—visit the Richmond Nature Park Society's Facebook page for listings. We recommend picking up the free bird and plant ID brochures here, along with the park guide and trail map that charts the expansive peat bog habitat waiting for you outside.

Don't hit the trails just yet, though. Immediately behind the Nature House, stop and take a seat. Several bird feeders are strategically placed here, and information panels profile exactly what you might see. We quickly spotted a rufous hummingbird—an annual visitor that arrives here every spring—before we continued on our way, starting with the wheelchair-accessible boardwalk Pond Trail.

The Nature Park—like much of Richmond—is a popular spot for geocaching, a cost-free scavenger-hunting pursuit where you use your phone to track down "treasure." Search online for Richmond GeoTour to find out more.

Nearby

- Paulik Neighbourhood Park (p. 68)
- Larry Berg Flight Path Park (p. 66)
- Richmond Cultural Centre (p. 70)

STEVESTON MUSEUM & POST OFFICE

M&H

3811 Moncton Street, Richmond

Head through the door beside the post office counter and you'll soon be unwrapping a large parcel of Steveston stories of yesteryear, including some that are tough to tell. The first room is lined with vintage village photos depicting Indigenous weavers, gossiping cannery workers and impressively moustachioed saloon drinkers. There's also a video tracing Steveston's roller coaster development.

That roller coaster takes a sharp turn in the adjoining Steveston Japanese Canadian Museum. Immigrants from Japan began working in BC's fishing sector in the 19th-century. By 1942, many multi-generational families had been living here for decades. That's when the wartime government forced thousands of Japanese Canadians into internment camps and seized their property—illustrated here by a jaw-dropping photo of countless confiscated fishing boats.

The museum provides a powerful account of what's now recognized as a shameful period in Canada's past. But there are also lots of exhibits that commemorate the positive contributions of Steveston's Japanese Canadian community before and after the war. Check out the displays on education and healthcare facilities, as well as a cabinet of everyday artifacts including a 1940s rice bag and 1950s fishing floats.

Our favourite exhibit, though, is the wall-mounted array of antique metal name signs that were used to identify fishing totes in a local cannery net loft. Dented and scuffed through repeated use, they bring to life the names of many Japanese Canadian families—Hamade, Urata, Yamamoto and more—who worked here long before most of us were born.

Nearby

- Britannia Shipyards National Historic Site (p. 63)
- Steveston Tram (p. 73)
- Freecouvering Around Steveston (p. 74)

STEVESTON TRAM

M&H

GFK

4011 Moncton Street, Richmond

On your next SkyTrain ride, spare a thought for a long-gone local transit network that was far more extensive—then head to Steveston and climb aboard. Housed in its own pavilion, the beautifully preserved Tramcar 1220 is a rare survivor (there's another in **Burnaby Village Museum, p. 96**) from an interurban tram system that had five major lines, travelled as far as Chilliwack and peaked at 141 million annual rides in the mid-1940s.

Loved by the kind of kids who count Thomas the Tank Engine as a close personal friend, a trip to the pavilion isn't just about hanging out with the jolly, red-painted tram. Junior visitors also enjoy the hands-on exhibits, transport-themed storybooks and dress-up corner, where they can transform into smartly attired conductors.

There's also plenty for nostalgic adults to get excited about, from a push-button map highlighting the old system's lines and stations to a fascinating timeline profiling Steveston–to–Vancouver travel options through the decades. These evolved from five-hour stagecoach trips to the BC Electric Railway's trams to the modern buses that killed off the tramcars in the 1950s.

The highlight of any visit, though, is the chance to hop aboard, slide onto a rattan-covered seat and imagine what riding the rails was really like. You'll find controls at each end of the car (the seats could also be reversed), newspaper racks where passengers shared reading materials and vintage adverts proclaiming the wonders of everything from Eaton's coffee to Nemo girdles. Those were the days!

The Tram offers special free family-friendly events throughout the year. Our favourite is Winter Tram, when the pavilion and its star attraction are fully decorated for the holidays.

Nearby

- Britannia Shipyards National Historic Site (p. 63)
- Steveston Museum & Post Office (p. 72)
- Freecouvering Around Steveston (p. 74)

FREECOUVERING . . . AROUND STEVESTON

The historic home of the West Coast fishing industry, Richmond's heritage village is a delightful destination at any time of the year. But while you're enjoying its independent stores and the top-notch fish and chips, save time for a relaxing roam around the shoreline.

Start at the **Steveston Cafe & Hotel (1)** at 3rd Avenue and Moncton Street. On the building's Moncton side is a mural depicting the 1889 arrival of the SV *Titania*. The first ship to transport local canned salmon to Europe, it turbocharged Steveston's fishing sector. Head up the incline to

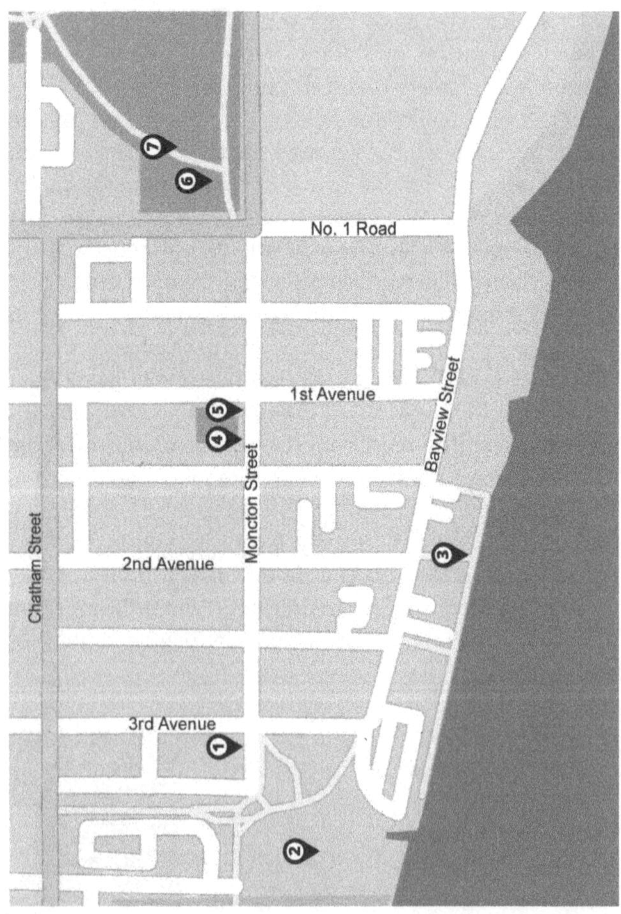

the **Gulf of Georgia Cannery National Historic Site (2)** to see how quickly things exploded.

Once BC's largest cannery, this Parks Canada property is free to visit on Canada Day; otherwise, it's well-worth dropping by if you have the budget. Outside the gabled, white-painted complex, you'll find an evocative sculpture entitled *Steveston's Legacy* showing three fishery workers engaged in animated conversation.

From here, head towards the waterfront, passing artwork recreations of vintage canned salmon labels. Then turn left along the boardwalk for a breezy shoreline saunter. Check out the fishing boats and pleasure cruisers, framed by the island-studded panorama. You'll soon reach the arched entrance to **Fisherman's Wharf (3)**.

Head down the ramp here and peruse the fresh catch for sale from the decks of the fishing boats. Snapper, geoduck and sea urchin are not unusual, but springtime spot prawns are the delicacy to look out for. Head back up the ramp and stroll straight down 2nd Avenue, turning right along Moncton Street.

You'll soon reach **Town Square Park (4)**, a small tree-lined green space with several heritage plaques. Look for the "Big Red Forever Remembered" granite marker commemorating a beloved dog that locals regarded as Steveston's unofficial mayor. Next door, you'll discover a wealth of human-based village history at the **Steveston Museum & Post Office (p. 72) (5).** Continue along Moncton until you reach the No. 1 Road intersection. Crossing to the small park, look for the **Nikkei Memorial (6)**. It marks the 75th anniversary of the wartime internment of Steveston's Japanese Canadians—and the fact that many of them returned to help rebuild the village. Also in the park is the **Steveston Tram (p. 73) (7)** that once trundled between Vancouver and Steveston, stopping at a long-gone station across the street.

Nearby

- Britannia Shipyards National Historic Site (p. 63)
- Steveston Tram (p. 73)
- Steveston Museum & Post Office (p. 72)

WALK RICHMOND

G&N

Various locations, Richmond

A friendly and inviting way to discover Richmond while also increasing your daily step-count, there's no need to reserve ahead for these sociable strolls. Peruse the schedule, then simply arrive at the appointed time and place for an outing suitable for all ages and fitness levels.

Operating year-round, whatever the weather, every month offers several walk options. Each lasts for an hour or so and everyone moves at their own pace—don't forget to wear good walking shoes, bring a water bottle and perhaps add a sunhat and sunscreen. The walks typically weave along well-marked trails and paths in local parks, greenway areas and shoreline swathes.

Popular routes such as Terra Nova, Finn Slough and South Dyke Trail are often repeated throughout the year, so don't worry if you miss one that you'd really like to try. Some walks are also specially designated for wheelchair users and dog walkers. Keep in mind that the organizers are always looking for volunteers to serve as walk leaders.

We recently joined the Garry Point Park/West Dyke Trail Walk, alongside around 30 other participants. Initially, our group circled the park's shoreline, spotting lots of birds and wildflowers en route. Then we connected to the dyke pathway, enjoying panoramic ocean views framed by distant peaks. By the end, we felt fully restored, as if we'd breathed deeply for the first time in weeks!

Freecouver Tip Go behind the scenes at Doors Open Richmond, an annual, weekend-long event (typically in June) where dozens of local museums, civic facilities, cultural organizations and more offer special tours, talks and more that showcase what they do—for free!

Surrey, Langley & White Rock

Freecouver Tips for Getting Around

We like to complain about it sometimes, but our transit network stretches far and wide throughout Greater Vancouver. In fact, we visited almost everything in this book via bus, SkyTrain or SeaBus, using TransLink's Trip Planner tool. Don't forget that weekends as well as weekdays after 6:30 pm are regarded as off-peak, which means all fares are treated as one-zone.

You can save even more money on transit by diving into TransLink's long list of special deals, from 2-for-1 admission to various attractions to discounts on dining. All you have to do is show your Compass Card or proof of same-day fare—a great way to save on your days out around the region.

Alternatively, cut you transportation costs to zero—unless you count calories as currency—by hopping in the saddle. Vancouver, Richmond, Burnaby and other communities have extensive cycling routes that can zip you around without having to pay a penny. These areas provide extensive maps and resources for cyclists.

You can even save money on the super-cute mini-ferries that operate in and around False Creek. Both Aquabus and False Creek Ferries offer a selection of day passes, bulk ticket deals and more. Speaking of passes: if you're planning a big day out with lots of Freecouvering stops along the way, consider a TransLink DayPass—but only if you're sure you'll save money compared to the regular fares.

Find out more at *freecouver.com*.

BARNSTON ISLAND FERRY

G&N

GFK

17775 104 Avenue, Surrey

About halfway across the Fraser River by ferry, we realized we were going to dock backwards, which meant putting the car into reverse, checking the mirrors, trusting the back-up camera and slowly bumping our way up the ramp onto Barnston Island. This is just how things work here.

It was our first lesson of the day. The second came soon after, when the many signs around the island made it clear that parking isn't allowed anywhere along the roadway. Tip: Use the generously sized parking lot on the Surrey Bend Park side of the crossing, then walk or cycle onto the free ferry (more of a barge propelled by a tugboat) that operates on demand. It's quick, it's fun, and it's a bit of a thrill.

Across the narrow channel, the island opens up into a quiet, rural landscape with a mix of private homes and working farms, along with two public parks tucked along the way. From the ferry landing, it's a 1.9-kilometre walk/ride to the first riverside picnic ground at Barnston Island Regional Park.

The island is flat, with the dyke road tracing its entire circumference. The full circle route around the island is under 10 kilometres. You'll ride past cows and cranberry bogs, views of the Golden Ears peaks across the river to the east, and the Port Mann Bridge to the west. In the picnic spots, the farthest being Mann Point (4.1 kilometres from the ferry) on the eastern tip facing Golden Ears Bridge, you can watch the river rush by, and spot migratory birds perching on log booms.

NOTE If you are planning to arrive by transit, keep in mind that the bus stop closest to the ferry terminal is a kilometre away.

Nearby

- Surrey Nature Centre (p. 90)
- Surrey Art Gallery (p. 89)

BC VINTAGE TRUCK MUSEUM

M&H
GFK

6022 176 Street, Surrey

The first thing you're asked here is if you'd like to sign the guest book. It's located next to a display case of T-shirts sporting the catchphrase "I still play with trucks." The second question is whether you'd like a guided tour—an offer well worth taking. Donations are appreciated but not required for entry or the tour.

The museum began 14 years ago with 22 trucks, and its collection has nearly doubled since. The focus is on trucks used in BC, including a few built here, with each vehicle telling a fascinating story beyond its own bumper. There's a BC Tel van, forestry trucks and gas pumps, and the first commercial truck to drive the Coquihalla Highway—a 1936 Model 87 Indiana. There's a 108-year-old wooden-cab FED Model B military service vehicle from the First World War that was later put to use by the BC Electric Railway, hauling coal and ploughing snow. The oldest in the collection is a 1910 White Steam Van with acetylene-powered headlights.

Each vehicle's sign details its make, model and year, along with how it was acquired, what it was used for and if it's appeared in any locally filmed movies or TV shows.

The steady hum of an air compressor reverberates throughout the patchwork of buildings as dedicated volunteers work on restorations. Their current project is a 1935 K52 Dodge Airflow made for Standard Oil Company, one of only a handful in existence. It looks like it's straight out of the pages of a Dick Tracy comic.

Our guide quipped that the old tools on the wall are less practical and handy today but make for nice museum displays. Even for those not into the mechanics of it all, the dioramas, LEGO and vintage photo albums of trucks, trams and carriages will reward any visitor's curiosity.

Nearby

- Museum of Surrey (p. 86)
- Honeybee Centre (p. 85)

DEREK DOUBLEDAY ARBORETUM

G&N

21177 Fraser Highway, Langley

Parked between a busy Fraser Valley highway and a regional airport, the Derek Doubleday Arboretum has roughly 8 hectares of flowering gardens, picnic areas, gravel walking trails and memorials.

Cared for by the Arboretum and Botanical Society of Langley, this former farm site has been consistently incorporating gardens and developing new features for years, thanks to donations from the community.

Stroll through the rose garden, the willow garden and the bird garden. Learn about natural dyes from plants in the Dyer's Garden, or sustainable food production in the Langley Demonstration Garden.

Along the north side, bordering Murray Creek, take note of some young oak trees. These were planted from acorns from Vimy Ridge on the 100th anniversary of the First World War battle in 1917. The Battle of Vimy Ridge, where four Canadian divisions became a unified fighting force for the first time, is commonly considered a turning point in Canadian history. Nearby, the *A Walk to Remember* art installation commemorates Canadian Forces personnel who lost their lives while serving in the Canadian mission in Afghanistan.

Sit and watch planes take off from the Langley Airport and admire the views of Mount Baker to the east. The arboretum is a very popular spot for dog walkers, picnickers and anyone who enjoys hearing the buzzing of bees on wildflowers, admiring perfectly pruned rhododendrons and feeling a cool breeze through a leafy canopy.

Freecouver Tip Inspired by trees? Check out the City of Vancouver's public tree registry to find the most Instagrammable groves.

Nearby

- Sendall Gardens (p. 88)
- Freecouvering Around Fort Langley (p. 82)

FREECOUVERING . . .
AROUND FORT LANGLEY

Stroll through a storybook village steeped in history when you spend an afternoon in Fort Langley village. Part of the Township of Langley, this community gets its name from the Hudson's Bay Company fort where BC was proclaimed a colony in 1858. Start at the **Fort Langley Community Hall (1)**, the picturesque yellow building that has been featured in many locally filmed movies and TV shows.

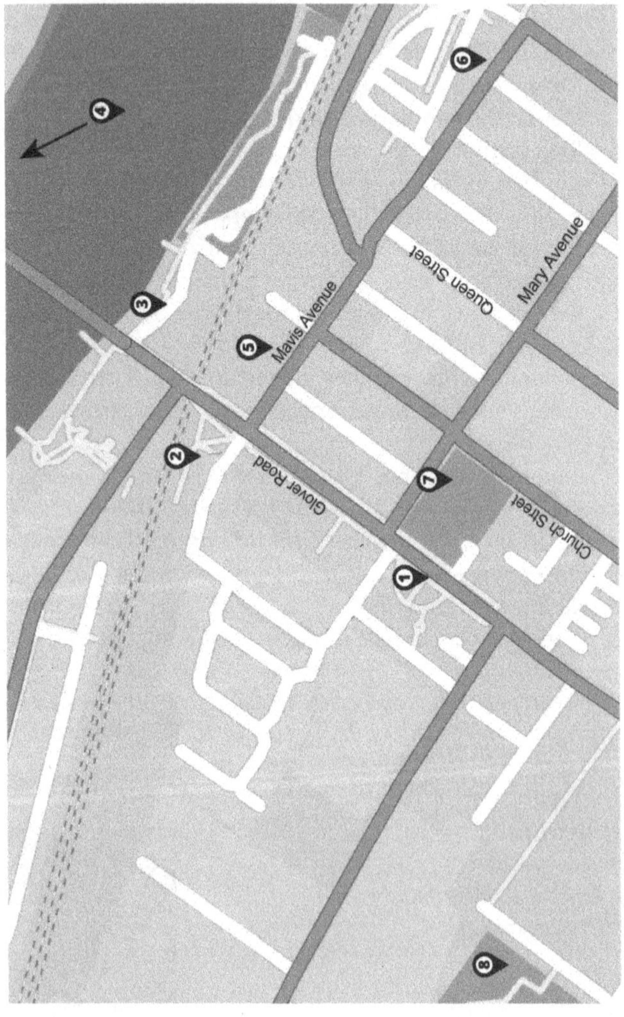

Continue up Glover Road to the 1915 **Historic CNR Station (2)** located along a busy railway still used to this day. The station has seasonal hours, but you can check out some classic railcars in its yard at any time of year. Still on Glover, cross the tracks and head to the river for a view of the Fraser, then step onto the **Fort to Fort Trail (3)** that connects Fort Langley with Derby Reach Regional Park along an 8-kilometre riverside path. Explore as much of the trail as you like on this visit or plan to come again. When you're done, cross the bridge over to **Brae Island Regional Park (4)**, a great spot for birding, cycling or walking on the paths, or watching rowers on the river.

Come back across the bridge on Glover and turn left onto Mavis Avenue. Visit the **Village Antique Mall (5)** that boasts 930 square metres of nostalgia-inducing kiosks packed with postcards, records, dishes, clothing, cameras and more, each presented like a museum display. Continue up Mavis to admire the art and architecture of the new **salishan Place by the River (6)**, home to the Fort Langley library. It's across from the namesake fort, a National Historic Site of Canada. Admission to the site is paid, except on Canada Day.

Loop back towards the village centre along King Street, turning right on Mary Avenue, and stop at the corner of Church Street. The **Pop-Up Park (7)** here has a great little playground and lawn, and it is the home of free festival events including the summertime Fort Langley Jazz Festival and the very popular Fort Langley Cranberry Festival held each October. Cross the park to get back onto Glover Road and you're back where you started at the white and yellow Fort Langley Community Hall. Brush on by or stop to take a photo when the decorated trees are out front during the holidays, then make your way to your last stop at **Fort Langley Park (8)**. From Glover, the first green space you'll encounter is the Fort Langley Cemetery, established in 1881. Behind it, the park has a playground shaded by tall Douglas firs, washroom facilities, spray park, soccer field and baseball diamond.

Nearby

- Derek Doubleday Arboretum (p. 81)
- Sendall Gardens (p. 88)

HISTORIC STEWART FARM

M&H

GFK

13723 Crescent Road, Surrey

Step into the life of a hardworking Surrey family from the 1900s, then kick back with a picnic in their riverside orchard. This historic farmhouse was built in 1894 for newcomers John and Annie Stewart and their two sons. Considered modest at the time, the two-storey house has a large footprint compared to local real estate today, or even heritage houses from the same era located in urban areas.

At its height, the Stewart property spanned 178 hectares, including the land visitors see today and additional farmland across the river. With the closest city at the time being New Westminster, roughly 30 kilometres away, the family farm had to be completely self-reliant.

Sip a cup of tea or coffee in the welcome centre at Stewart Hall before walking across the gravel lot to the main attraction. Turn the doorknob and you'll be promptly greeted by a staff member dressed in period-appropriate attire who will give you the lay of the land: a sitting room, dining room and parlour, as well as a large kitchen.

While the wallpaper, furniture and finishings in its rooms are later additions chosen to match the period, try to spot the one item genuinely belonging to the original owners— the Stewart family Bible. Hint: It's a magnificent volume, roughly the size of a small calf.

The wrap-around verandah offers views of the additional buildings at the heritage site including the barn and the picnic area. It's a charming window into 19th-century farm life, and the everyday world of the Stewarts.

While you're there, stop into the Totest Aleng: Indigenous Learning House. This open air studio acts as a workshop for artists in residence and as a venue for occasional free public programs.

Nearby

- White Rock Museum & Pier (p. 91)
- Redwood Park (p. 87)

HONEYBEE CENTRE

G&N

GFK

7480 176 Street, Surrey

The barn on the corner of Fraser Highway and 176 Street, Surrey's old Fry's Corner, is buzzing with activity. This farm-stand gift shop celebrates all things honey, and you can get a free education on these pollinators when you stop by to browse.

Between the rows of beeswax, bee plushies, soaps, candles and creams, there are dozens of types of honey, each with informative signage explaining how it flows from flower to jar. Have you ever wondered why some honey gets hard, sugary or foggy? The display about crystallization will tell you all you need to know (and no, it's not expired; it's a sign the honey is real and raw).

There's cocoa, cardamom or habanero infused honeys, bourbon barrel-aged and traditional clover or wildflower. Kids can explore colourful bee-themed books and toys, and the centre has an indoor hive, housed under a plexiglass dome with a tube leading outside, where you can safely get up close with these busy, buzzy workers. The store has community hives all over Surrey and Langley, including some in the orchard at **Historic Stewart Farm (p. 84)**. There is a fee for their workshops and field trips, but they also have free drop-in programming in their outdoor education centre on occasion. Major events, like their World Bee Day celebration in May, are also free to attend. Follow their beekeepers' account on Instagram (honeybeecentrekids) for information on specific events.

Freecouver Tip Surrey, once known as the City of Parks, has 100 kilometres of nature trails with heritage forests, winding creeks, and world-class birding. From Bear Creek to Hi-Knoll, we've linked them all on our website.

Nearby

- BC Vintage Truck Museum (p. 80)
- Museum of Surrey (p. 86)

MUSEUM OF SURREY

M&H

GFK

17710 - 56A Avenue, Surrey

Children run and laugh, eager to dash back to a quick game of pick-up hockey after rehydrating in the lobby. But this isn't the local rec centre—it's the Museum of Surrey, currently showcasing the season's "Our Connection to Hockey" exhibit in their rotating Feature Gallery. A vibrant museum complete with an indoor treehouse, slide and "scarf cannon," it hosts both temporary and permanent collections on its campus.

Step inside the Surrey Stories Gallery upstairs to find the neon Rickshaw sign, a poster for the Clova Theatre, a nod to Two EE's market and a family photo album that might spark a wave of nostalgia, whether or not you grew up here. From farming and first responders to Vaisakhi celebrations and even a 1950s living room, you'll discover artifacts and memorabilia tracing Surrey's past and present—a city shaped by forests, railroads, highways, rivers and merging cultures.

In the Indigenous Hall, q̓icə̓y̓ (Katzie), q̓ʷɑ:n̓ƛ̓ən̓ (Kwantlen), and se'mya'me (Semiahmoo) Nations are invited to represent their histories and stories and share other Indigenous narratives. During our visit, the gallery was filled with cedar weaving, paintings, beading and quilts from Indigenous artists.

In the Community Treasure Gallery, we read personal narratives in "Journeys in Care: Stories from Nurses of Indian Heritage." Overall, this lively museum (where donations are welcome) not only reflects on how the city was shaped; it also celebrates the diversity and voices that make Surrey vibrant today.

Outside, you'll find several heritage buildings, including the 1881 Town Hall structure and the Anniedale School, built in 1891 and moved to the Museum's yard in 2018.

Nearby

- BC Vintage Truck Museum (p. 80)
- Honeybee Centre (p. 85)

REDWOOD PARK

G&N

GFK

17900 - 20th Avenue, Surrey

Groves of European ash, Norway spruce, Sierra Redwoods, and Wych elm are not the trees you typically find in the Pacific Northwest, where Western red cedars, Douglas firs, and alders dominate the landscape. This makes Redwood Park a truly unique place to explore.

The story begins with two brothers who, in 1893, received a large plot of land from their father. Rather than turning it into farmland, as he had hoped, the brothers filled the vast space with their favourite trees from around the world. Fully committed to their forest sanctuary, the eccentric duo even built a treehouse, where they lived in solitude until their deaths in 1949 and 1958.

Today, their arboretum forms the heart of Redwood Park, complete with a playground, picnic areas, and over 5 kilometres of walking trails, allowing visitors to wander among the very trees the brothers once cherished.

The park features a replica of the brothers' treehouse and their collection of trees, each with a collar that provides its name and description. It's one of the most unique places for spring blossoms and fall foliage in Metro Vancouver because of the diversity of its canopy. It's also home to some of the tallest monkey puzzle trees we've ever seen. Usually ornamental, the spiky limbs of these national trees of Chile tower over the forest alongside majestic sequoias.

A visit to Redwood Park feels like a tree treasure hunt—don't forget to look up!

> **Freecouver Tip** The City of Surrey's Our City Workshop series offers free hands-on learning to build skills and knowledge to improve your neighbourhood, from tree pruning to protecting pollinators.

Nearby

- Historic Stewart Farm (p. 84)
- White Rock Museum & Pier (p. 91)

SENDALL GARDENS

G&N

GFK

20166 50 Avenue, Langley

A miniature—and free—take on some of BC's finest curated gardens sits tucked into a residential neighbourhood in Langley, complete with a few surprises, including banana trees.

Sendall Gardens is just shy of 1.6 hectares, but it packs in an impressive number of unique features, from a fountain on a hill that cascades into a little waterfall to stone staircases that lead to a creek flowing through a ravine lined with colourful flower beds.

Boardwalks and wooden bridges wind through the trees, while rhododendrons and other flowering shrubs encircle picnic tables. In the summer, every branch, bloom and draping vine spills over the arbours, framing the gazebo in a scene worthy of a Monet canvas and making it a popular backdrop for graduation and wedding photos. Sit on a bench under a flowering magnolia stellata and listen to the calming trickle of the waterfall.

Take a contemplative stroll around the labyrinth and pop into the tropical greenhouse that's open to the public from April to October. Sliding open the massive door, the humidity might fog your glasses as pink and orange flowers come into focus, piercing the lush green landscape packed with plants you rarely see north of the 49th parallel, just around the corner from someone's backyard.

As you leave the gardens, you can head north on 201A Street for a couple of blocks to the Nicomekl Trail, a greenway of walking and bike paths that meander over bridges and along the walkways of Langley's floodplain. The trail is about 5 kilometres long but you will intersect it near its midpoint. Turn left to head toward Brydon Lagoon or right toward Portage Park.

Nearby

- Derek Doubleday Arboretum (p. 81)
- Freecouvering Around Fort Langley (p. 82)

SURREY ART GALLERY

A&E

GFK

13750 88 Avenue, Surrey

As you walk, roll or ride by the busy intersection of King George Boulevard and 88th Avenue in Surrey, look for a marker on the corner announcing, "You have entered a Surrey Art Spot," one of multiple signs and sidewalk stickers placed at culturally important sites to commemorate the 50th anniversary of the City's support for performing, literary and visual art.

Turn into the entrance to Bear Creek Park, primarily known for its athletic facilities and forest trails, and you'll reach the Surrey Arts Centre building, which houses the Surrey Art Gallery alongside the Surrey Civic Theatre's main stage and studio theatre.

The Surrey Art Gallery hosts exhibitions featuring contemporary art by local, national and international artists that rotate every 3-4 months. Each exhibition is paired with free workshops and events. We visited during "In the Shadow of the Pavilions: Expo 86 and Contemporary Art." Combining original artworks, audio and visual elements with archival materials, this is the first exhibition to closely examine Vancouver's defining world's fair through its art.

The gallery provides an Art Explorer Guide full of games and activities for kids and Art Thinker cards that spark reflection in adults. Drop by for an afternoon of artmaking during regularly scheduled Family Art Jams or attend one of the monthly artist talks hosted each month by the Surrey Art Gallery Association (SAGA).

The building itself has murals on the outside, and its corridors are filled with exhibits from local artists and elementary school students. Between the art gallery's main exhibition hall and the reception hall, duck outside the double doors to enjoy a quiet garden space with a water feature and additional sculptures.

Nearby

- Barnston Island Ferry (p. 79)
- Surrey Nature Centre (p. 90)

SURREY NATURE CENTRE

G&N

GFK

14225 Green Timbers Way, Surrey

Located on the edge of the 226-hectare Green Timbers Urban Forest, the Surrey Nature Centre shares the history of BC's first forest plantation, established after massive clearcuts at the turn of the 20th century, while also educating future generations about our local forest ecosystems.

Follow a paved path flanked by fragrant flowers and buzzing bees past restored buildings that date to the 1930s, when Surrey began replacing the old-growth timber harvested around the province. A timeline behind the reception desk informed us that Vancouver's Stanley Park received 3,000 saplings from Green Timbers in the 1930s to kickstart its own regrowth.

The Nature Centre has a reception area, a classroom and an interactive ecology exhibition space. The theme rotates every three months; during our visit, we learned about local bird species and got up close with displays of nests, feathers and hummingbird eggs as small as Tic Tacs. A microscope helped us examine every dimple on a Douglas fir cone and the fuzziest bits of a piece of green lichen on a twig.

Outside, the section of the 10-kilometre Green Timbers' trail network that loops around the Nature Centre features an arboretum with labelled trees, similar to the collars we spotted at **Redwood Park (p. 87)**. Winding gravel paths lead from meadows to sheltered forest trails, and you're never too far from a picnic table.

You can join a free guided nature walk on Saturdays or sit in on nature storytime on Wednesdays.

On your next outing, bring your rod and reel to try your hand at fishing in nearby Green Timbers Lake. It's open year-round for fishing from the shore and is stocked with rainbow trout from the Fraser Valley Hatchery.

Nearby

- Barnston Island Ferry (p. 79)
- Surrey Art Gallery (p. 89)

WHITE ROCK MUSEUM & PIER

M&H

GFK

14970 Marine Drive, White Rock

Take a stroll out onto Canada's longest pier, a 470-metre-long structure that juts out into Semiahmoo Bay. It was built in 1914, restored in 1977 and repaired from windstorm damage in 2019. When you reach the breakwater at the end, where crabbers pull up traps of Dungeness, you'll be rewarded with views of the colourful buildings dotting the hillside above the beach, while across the water (and the international boundary) lies Blaine, Washington.

The namesake white rock is just down the beach to the east of the pier, a remnant from the last ice age. The granite boulder, which is touched up regularly with a spot of paint, is over 4 metres high and weighs about 440 tonnes.

Follow the promenade that runs along the beach to the old railroad station, now home to the White Rock Museum & Archives. Donations for entry are welcome but not required. Inside you'll find a gift shop, rotating gallery exhibit, and a permanent collection that shares stories from the se'mya'me (Semiahmoo) First Nation, the city, and the first railway line linking Vancouver with Washington State in 1891. A display featuring the words of Grand Chief Bernard Charles shares the legend of the white rock, known as *P'Quals* among the se'mya'me people.

Tap along to the rhythm of the telegraph in the replica office. The Thomas the Tank Engine display will delight younger visitors. Every now and then, crossing bells will ring. Next comes a rumble and shadows flickering past the windows—it's the Amtrak Cascade en route from Vancouver to Seattle.

Outside the museum, pose with Denis Kleine's *Passenger*, a bronze statue of a man waiting for a train with a suitcase at his feet. Then and now, this modest museum hums with history and curiosity.

Nearby

- Historic Stewart Farm (p. 84)
- Redwood Park (p. 87)

Freecouver Tips for Entertainment

From alfresco concerts to street festivals and from cultural performances to pop-up events, there's a toe-tapping playbill of ongoing free entertainment running in our region all the time. The trick is to know when and where to go. Need a heads-up? Our website has a monthly hotlist of upcoming events to add to your calendar.

Need more? Visit the Vancouver Public Library's website for gratis happenings—from live music to author talks and much more—staged at branches throughout the city. You'll also find regular free concerts at the **Vancouver Academy of Music (p. 52)** and **UBC Roy Barnett Recital Hall (p. 50)** as well as at the legendary summer-long **Kitsilano Showboat (p. 25)**.

Film fan? Every summer, free outdoor movies are screened across the region—and all you have to do is show up. Locations change every year, but venues have recently included Stanley Park, the Vancouver Art Gallery, Richmond's Lansdowne Centre and North Vancouver's Lower Lonsdale area.

But perhaps the best way to experience an amazing event up-close without having to pay is to volunteer. Much-loved happenings such as Bard on the Beach, the Vancouver Folk Music Festival, the Vancouver International Jazz Festival and many more love their volunteers—and they offer great packages (including free shows) for your efforts.

Find out more at *freecouver.com*.

Burnaby & New Westminster

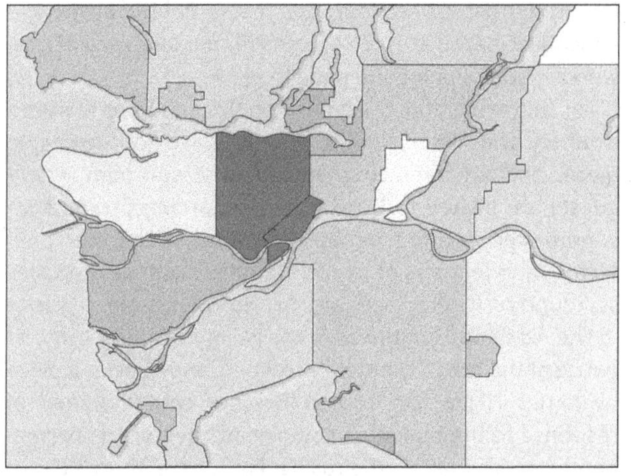

BURNABY ART GALLERY

A&E

GFK

6344 Deer Lake Avenue, Burnaby

Overlooking Deer Lake, the Burnaby Art Gallery (BAG) is housed inside the Arts and Crafts-style Fairacres Mansion. Since 1967, the gallery has been the only public art museum in Canada dedicated to collecting works of art on paper.

A donation of $10.00 is suggested but not required. We recommend you stop by the office to pick up a free, self-guided audio tour featuring commentary from the featured artist. During our visit, it was Bobbie Burgers, a Vancouver-based artist celebrated for her large-scale floral works made of paint and paper.

For this exhibition, the gallery on the first floor featured a variety of works, including an impressive floor-to-ceiling piece, and an interactive station in a sunroom where guests are invited to build their own artwork using supplied materials and magnets. Pause to admire the architecture and features of this 1911 manor, with painted tiles surrounding its fireplaces and Art Nouveau stained glass.

The exhibition continues in the gallery upstairs, but first pause at the top of the staircase where *Shù7mayus,* a piece by James Harry and Lauren Brevner commissioned in response to the building's colonial architecture, is permanently installed along the railing. From here, there's also a striking view of the leaded windows.

Free drop-in programs help guests do a deeper dive into the theme of each rotating exhibition. The gallery also offers a handout with a fun scavenger hunt for younger visitors that will help them engage with the pieces.

Freecouver Tip Enjoy free entertainment in Burnaby's Confederation Park throughout July and August as part of Summer Stages.

Nearby

- Burnaby Village Museum (p. 96)
- Nikkei National Museum & Cultural Centre (p. 104)

BURNABY MOUNTAIN CONSERVATION AREA

G&N
A&E
GFK

800 Burnaby Mountain Parkway, Burnaby

Offering some of the best panoramic views of Vancouver, the Burnaby Mountain Conservation Area is more than just a lookout. Home to walking trails, a rose garden, a playground and a picnic area, it's also where you can find a striking collection of sculptures that celebrate goodwill across the globe.

The wooden poles at Kamui Mintara (Playground of the Gods) might resemble Coast Salish totem carvings but they actually hail from the other side of the Pacific. Created by sculptors Nuburi Toko and his son, Shusei, members of Japan's Indigenous Ainu people, the cedar pieces commemorate the sister city relationship between Burnaby and Kushiro, Japan.

Telling a story of people, gods and creatures living on the earth, and the harmony of all things in nature, carvings atop the poles depict Ainu gods incarnated as animals including bears, owls and orcas. The smaller poles represent people. Unveiled in 1990 to mark the 20th anniversary of the cities' bond, the site boasts more than a dozen poles, each reaching skyward against the backdrop of Vancouver's glittering glass towers in the distance.

Time, weather, and the occasional curious climber looking for a photo op have taken a toll on the sculptures that were temporarily fenced off for assessment and preservation during our visit. But you'll still get the full effect from a distance.

The park features views of Burrard Inlet and Deep Cove, curated gardens, and cherry blossom trees flanking the main paths. Standing there on the mountain top with pink petal confetti blowing in the springtime definitely feels like heaven.

Nearby

- Gibson Art Museum (p. 98)
- Museum of Archaeology & Ethnology (p. 100)

BURNABY VILLAGE MUSEUM

M&H

GFK

6501 Deer Lake Avenue, Burnaby

The walk score for this small replica town near Deer Lake is a perfect 100. At Burnaby Village Museum, a historic main street unfolds with a general store, optometrist, bakery and barber shop—an entire past you can wander and explore on a 4-hectare site.

Catch a black-and-white movie in the one-room Central Park Theatre or sit in on a game of mahjong at the Way Sang Yuen Wat Kee Herbalist. Pop a coin into the box at Treble Clef Phonographs to activate the player-piano, then cross Main Street and watch a blacksmith forge a horseshoe. The Indigenous Learning House offers storytime on Tuesdays, Thursdays and Saturdays. On summer weekends, participate in Heritage Games in the meadow.

In the Tram Barn, hop aboard the restored (1912) Interurban Tram #1223 (cousin of the **Steveston Tram, p. 73)** that once ran from Burnaby to Chilliwack on a regular schedule. Experience how people used to travel through the region, when rides meant horsehair-filled seat cushions, intricate brass fittings and woodwork, and even a smoking section in the car.

For a small fee, visitors can ride a 1912 C.W. Parker Carousel, purchased and restored by a dedicated group of local citizens who raised $330,000 for the cause.

There are two historic houses on site: Elworth (1922) and the Love Farmhouse, one of the oldest surviving buildings in Burnaby, originally built in 1893 and later brought to the site.

Activated each year for Spring Break, then from May to September, and again for the Christmas holiday season, admission is free. There is an admission fee for their ticketed Haunted Halloween offering in the fall.

Nearby

- Burnaby Art Gallery (p. 94)
- Nikkei National Museum & Cultural Centre (p. 104)

GALLERY AT QUEEN'S PARK

A&E

Centennial Lodge, Queen's Park, New Westminster

Surrounded by soccer pitches, baseball diamonds, an arena and a skatepark, a quieter, softer scene unfolds on the top floor of Centennial Lodge in Queen's Park. Established in 1985, the one-room gallery hosts a steady rotation of a dozen exhibitions each year, spanning painting, sculpture and mixed media by artists from across Metro Vancouver. It's as much a community hub as an exhibition space, supporting emerging and established artists, with the occasional artist-in-residence added to the mix.

When we visited, the gallery was showcasing pieces from the preschool downstairs in an exhibition called *Imprints*, sharing how children observed the ways in which pressure, light and colour can change materials and create unique impressions. There were impressions from park flowers and plants, cyanotypes of cedar and ferns, and painted paper butterflies suspended from the ceiling.

There is no admission fee but donations to the New West Arts Council are welcome. The council also operates the City Hall Community Gallery, Amelia Douglas Gallery located on the 4th floor of Douglas College, and the Anvil Community Art Gallery on the third floor of the Anvil Centre (home of the **Museum of New Westminster, p. 101**) that showcases emerging and established local artists via rotating exhibitions throughout the year.

Pair your visit with a wander through the surrounding park along shaded walking trails or toward the nearby spray park on a hot summer's day. In May, you can watch local students dance around a Maypole, the longest-running such event in the Commonowealth (156 years and counting). In December, the lodge hosts a holiday market.

Nearby

- Irving House (p. 99)
- Museum of New Westminster (p. 101)
- Freecouvering Around the New Westminster Waterfront (p. 102)

GIBSON ART MUSEUM

A&E

**SFU Burnaby Campus,
8888 University Drive, Burnaby**

Opened in 2025 and committed to making art accessible to all, this bright and inviting gallery is a breath of fresh air. Step inside and you'll typically discover several pocket-sized exhibitions populating its multiple spaces, ranging from works from the extensive SFU art collection to visiting exhibits that might be here for just a few weeks.

On our visit, we were beguiled by Cindy Mochizuki's *Arboreal Time*. It's a large wood and ceramic installation featuring dozens of ethereal Japanese kodama spirits peeking from the branches of ancient trees. Use the printed map to help you track down Baby Tengu, Lucky Jinmenju and more, then snap some photos of your favourite folkloric beings.

Then explore the rest of the gallery, where you might encounter chin-stroking works in video, photography, multimedia sculpture and beyond. The trick is to slow down and immerse yourself in some unfamiliar ideas. There's also a well-curated gift shop here where you can pick up some great art books and cool prezzies for all the cultured people in your life.

Interactivity is a huge modus operandi at the Gibson and the gallery hosts regular free show openings, art talks and special events. And if you're inspired to get creative yourself, they also offer gratis workshops and drop-in Saturday events for a wide range of ages and abilities in their Tuey Art Studio space, materials and guidance provided.

The SFU art collection comprises more than 6,000 works, and hundreds of these are currently on display in campus buildings. Check their website to learn more.

Nearby

- Museum of Archaeology & Ethnology (p. 100)
- Burnaby Mountain Conservation Area (p. 95)

IRVING HOUSE

M&H

GFK

302 Royal Avenue, New Westminster

The closest thing to a palace you'll find in the Royal City is Irving House museum, built in 1865 as the home of William Irving, aka the "King of the River." One of the earliest captains on the Fraser River, Irving built a steamship empire at the time of the Gold Rush. The Gothic Revival home is one of the oldest community heritage sites in BC, and the oldest intact residence (still on its original land) in the Lower Mainland. Although the front of the house faces bustling Royal Avenue, along its side is a tranquil garden with blossoming trees and cool breezes.

Donations are appreciated but not required when you visit the almost 465-square-metre heritage home, which is open to visitors on weekends. Inside, you'll find 14 furnished rooms filled with an extensive collection of Victorian antiques, many of which are original to the residence.

Admire the ornate ceilings and plasterwork, and embellishments such as carpets, metallic gold wallpapers and fireplaces that were added onto the house when one of Irving's daughters undertook renovations in later years.

With the parlour and dining room all set for entertaining, you can fancy yourself a guest among the elaborate place settings, fine china and art. Kids can see the toys, games, dolls and clothing that the Irving children had in their bedrooms at the turn of the 20th century. There are also modern-day colouring sheets and crayons on offer to engage young visitors.

Stand in the footsteps of William Irving in front of the lofty windows along the east side of the house, where he would watch his fleet sail up and down the river.

Nearby

- Gallery at Queen's Park (p. 97)
- Museum of New Westminster (p. 101)
- Freecouvering Around the New Westminster Waterfront (p. 102)

MUSEUM OF ARCHAEOLOGY & ETHNOLOGY

M&H

SFU Burnaby Campus,
8888 University Drive, Burnaby

Tucked inside the Escher-like labyrinth of Simon Fraser University buildings, you'll know you've finally found this museum when you spot the towering *Frog Constellation* carving guarding its entrance. Take your time photographing this dramatic Jim Hart creation from every angle, then head inside to discover a kaleidoscopic array of additional enthralling exhibits.

Like a mini version of UBC's Museum of Anthropology, Indigenous poles, masks and house posts from communities such as the 'Namgis, Tsimshian and Nuu-chah-nulth dominate this high-ceilinged, one-room gallery. Slow down for the full immersive effect: you'll find petroglyphs from Lillooet, an amazing sea wolf mask from Alert Bay and a Salish house post with shimmering abalone eyes and a supernatural backstory.

The museum doesn't only focus on Indigenous communities close to home, though. There are also artifact displays from overseas, including evocative masks from Africa and a row of wooden shields—topped with carved heads—from New Guinea. Fashioned from mango tree root, each head represents an ancestor from the Asmat community who helps fortify the owner of the shield.

Before you leave, save time to peruse the informative exhibit on radiocarbon dating techniques along with 17th-century cabinets of curiosity, the forerunners of modern-day museums. Then, if the weather is amenable, head out to explore the wider campus in search of photo-ready indoor and outdoor works created by celebrated Indigenous artists such as Bill Reid and Susan Point.

Nearby

- Burnaby Mountain Conservation Area (p. 95)
- Gibson Art Museum (p. 98)

MUSEUM OF NEW WESTMINSTER

M&H

Anvil Centre, 777 Columbia Street, New Westminster

This surprisingly spacious third-floor museum illuminates New Westminster's development from its Indigenous foundations through its tumultuous pioneer era to its 20th-century challenges. Along the way, you'll find unexpected stories, fascinating characters and an eclectic array of engaging artifacts.

Originally called Queensborough when the Brits chose it as the capital of their British Columbia colony in 1859, Western Canada's first city was soon renamed New Westminster. But when BC and the colony of Vancouver Island were later amalgamated, it lost out to Victoria as the region's top metropolis. Did the city ever recover from this snub? Let's just say it took a different turn.

Exploring the museum, you'll find charred remnants of the city's 1898 Great Fire alongside huge photos of bustling streetcar scenes and massive May Day parades. Cool vehicle exhibits include the carriage used by Canada's Governor General to tour BC in 1876. It's next to a shiny Model-T Ford once owned by a local man—check out the story of what happened when he faced down a locomotive in it!

It's easy to linger over these exhibits, but don't miss the museum's unexpected bonus area. The Canadian Lacrosse Hall of Fame showcases North America's oldest team sport. You can read about its Indigenous origins before plunging into a dazzling nostalgia fest of trophies, memorabilia and vintage jerseys from local teams including the New Westminster Salmonbellies, a storied team that continues to command a devoted following.

After you exit, check out the Community Art Gallery, also located on the Anvil Centre's third floor.

Nearby

- Irving House (p. 99)
- Gallery at Queen's Park (p. 97)
- Freecouvering Around the New Westminster Waterfront (p. 102)

FREECOUVERING . . . AROUND THE NEW WESTMINSTER WATERFRONT

Bridges, mountains, trains, murals and a whole lot of local history await you on the New Westminster waterfront that parallels the Fraser River. Start on Columbia Street and check out the **Fourth Street Stairs and Mural (1)**, which provide an engaging way to get down to Front Street. Admire them from above, then take the pedestrian overpass, with its views of train tracks and bridges, including the SkyTrain's soaring SkyBridge.

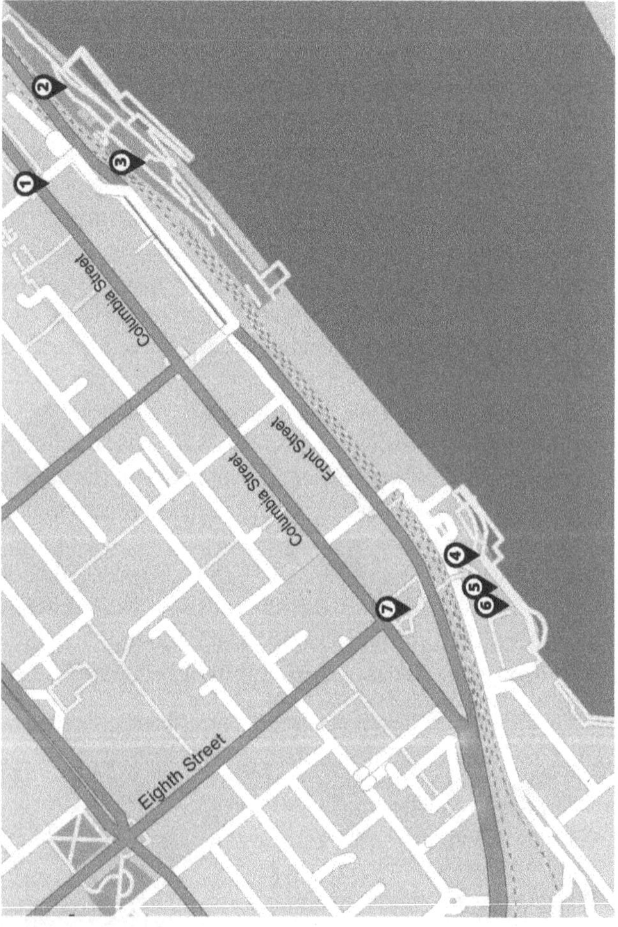

From the overpass, take the elevator or stairs down to **Westminster Pier Park (2)**, a waterfront boardwalk with a festival lawn, lounge chairs, elevated seating areas and even a few hammocks. Before you reach one of the many playgrounds, pause to view the public art piece ***Community on the River: The Place Where People Meet at Lytton Square*** **(3)**. It's located under the skeleton of a large, timber-frame structure that pays tribute to the old Lytton Square market building that once stood in this area. The playgrounds have plenty of river-themed parts to pull, push, climb and swing. The "pile forests" along the boardwalk make you feel like you're walking under the pier as a wavy green lawn mimics the movement of the river.

Continue your stroll and you won't be able to miss the **World's Tallest Tin Soldier (4)**, modelled after a sergeant major of the Royal Engineers' Columbia Detachment. It stands guard in front of the New Westminster Quay's River Market, home to an eclectic collection of shops and eateries. The upper floor houses the Vancouver Circus School, which regularly hosts free circus days for the whole family. Pre-registration is required.

On the boardwalk outside the market is a bronze bust of fur trader **Simon Fraser (5)**, the river's namesake, and the ***Samson V*** **(6)**, docked off the pier. It's the last surviving wooden steam-powered sternwheeler, built in 1937. During the summer season, you can board this floating museum for free.

Loop back past the Tin Soldier and take the pedestrian overpass up over the tracks once more to the ***Wait for Me Daddy Sculpture*** **(7)**, based on a photo that became one of the most iconic Canadian images of the Second World War. It depicts the British Columbia Regiment (Duke of Connaught's Own Rifles) marching down Eighth Street at the Columbia Street intersection and a child who broke free from his mother to run and catch up with his father, who was shipping off to war in 1940.

Nearby

- Irving House (p. 99)
- Museum of New Westminster (p. 101)
- Gallery at Queen's Park (p. 97)

NIKKEI NATIONAL MUSEUM & CULTURAL CENTRE

M&H

6688 Southoaks Crescent, Burnaby

This landmark, purpose-built facility offers an immersive introduction to the history and modern-day vibrancy of Japanese Canadian culture. You'll encounter that vibrancy as soon as you enter the lobby, where chatty dance, sports and community groups gather to wait for their activities to start. Weave through the crowd and climb the staircase to find the centre's permanent museum exhibit.

Deploying yesteryear photos, information panels and poignant quotations, the corridor galleries here bring to life the tumultuous story of the Japanese Canadian community. From the late-1800s arrival of the first immigrants to gritty jobs in farming, mining, logging and fishing—look for the photo of cannery workers with babies on their backs—it wasn't long before discrimination reared up.

That prejudice peaked in 1942 when the Canadian government interned thousands of Japanese Canadians, seizing their homes and property. The museum profiles BC's New Denver internment camp, where 1,700 men, women and children were held in cramped cabins and forced to work on beet farms, with parents binding their kids' hands to protect them.

After the war, some families returned (many chose not to), but formal redress wasn't offered until 1988. By then, the community had long been rebuilding itself, and the museum depicts many modern-day Japanese Canadians becoming MPs, MLAs and more. Conclude your visit in the lobby level's Karasawa Gallery, where temporary exhibitions are staged—on our visit, it was a colourful show about Vancouver's much-loved Powell Street Festival, complete with vintage posters, archive videos and the chance to try on some wearable sushi!

Nearby

- Burnaby Art Gallery (p. 94)
- Burnaby Village Museum (p. 96)

North Shore

North Vancouver

West Vancouver

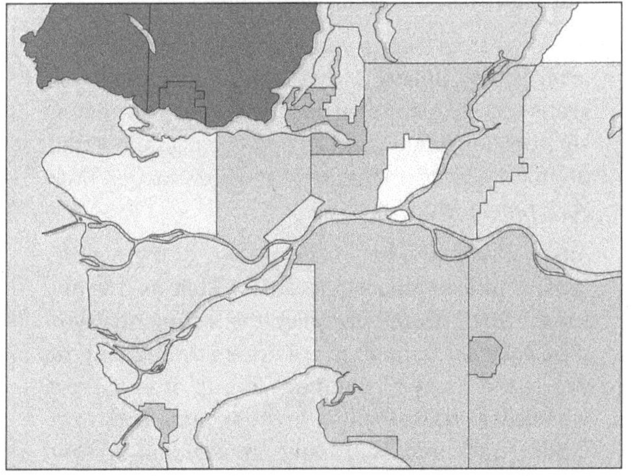

Freecouver Tips for Recreation

If you have your own wheels, consider a Circle Farm Tour in the Fraser Valley. There are four free downloadable map tours that point you to warm and welcoming producers in Abbotsford, Agassiz and Harrison Mills, Chilliwack and Langley.

If the weather keeps you indoors, check our your local library online. Most library cards gives you gratis access to a host of cool resources—streaming services, language courses and the digital editions of hundreds of magazines and newspaper (*New York Times* included).

Alternatively, why not check out one of the region's most impressive sports facilities? Built as a venue for the 2010 Winter Olympics, the Richmond Olympic Oval hosts a multitude of events throughout the year—and many of them are free to attend. From wheelchair basketball to martial arts, and from indoor track and field meets to regional or even national gymnastics championships, check their calendar to see what's coming up.

Vancouver is also a hotbed of Little Free Libraries, where you can browse and select books (and sometimes more) that locals are giving away. The hugely popular program's website has a searchable map that pinpoints all the locations around the region.

Find out more at *freecouver.com*.

CLEVELAND DAM & CAPILANO RIVER REGIONAL PARK

G&N

5077 Capilano Road, North Vancouver

Nothing will wake you up for a morning hike faster than standing atop a dam after an atmospheric river, as a billion litres of drinking water thunder down the spillway toward the city.

Vancouver's pristine drinking water starts as rain and snowmelt, and you can visit where it's gathered at Capilano River Regional Park, home to the Cleveland Dam and Capilano Watershed.

The views of Capilano, Crown, Fromme and Grouse Mountains are worth the visit alone. The park offers picnic areas, forest trails and dramatic granite canyon views above the winding Capilano River, where rainforest and river converge in awe-inspiring fashion.

The mechanics of the whole operation are just as captivating, from the Capilano Valve Chamber by the main parking lot to interpretive signage that traces the reservoir's history to the Cleveland Dam, which the public can walk across. Explore the inner workings of this complex system while soaking up the scenery as trails continue on the far side of the dam, inviting you to follow the river through the winding canyon and experience the journey of our drinking water from every angle.

If you do venture close to the water, watch for flashing signals and sirens that warn when the floodgates are about to change pressure; the river level can rise quickly. For this reason, no boating, swimming or wading is allowed in the river. Besides, it's good to keep your boots out of this sensitive salmon habitat, which will eventually flow into your drinking glass.

Down river, we can't wait until the Capilano River Hatchery returns in 2030 after the rebuild that began in 2026.

Nearby

- Lynn Canyon Suspension Bridge (p. 110)

FREECOUVERING . . .
AROUND LOWER LONSDALE

Start your exploration on the **Shoreline Deck (1)** outside North Vancouver's renamed Quay Market & Food Hall (still known by most of us as Lonsdale Quay Market). It provides breathtaking views of downtown Vancouver, shimmering on the other side of Burrard Inlet. Snap some scenic panoramas, especially if a SeaBus vessel edges into the frame.

Next, walk through the market, pausing at the mosaic floor mural of trees and ravens at the building's north end. Exit here and you'll glimpse the silvery sawtooth roof of the

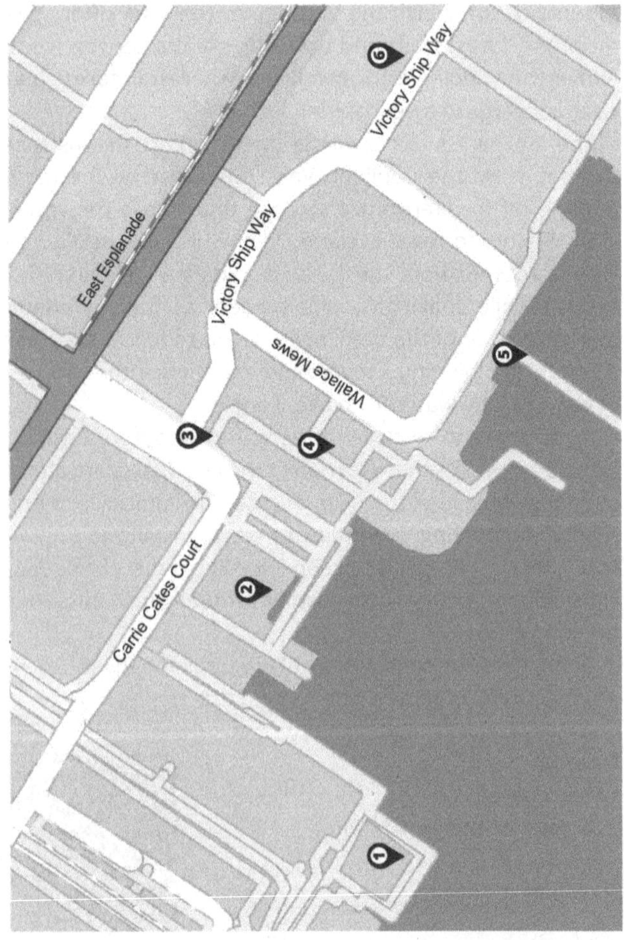

nearby **Polygon Gallery (2).** Turn right along Carrie Cates Court and you'll soon be there. Admission is by donation (suggested $15.00) but you can admire some artwork in the lobby and check out the excellent gift shop.

Back outside, cross to the huge Tap & Barrel restaurant. On the building's left edge, you'll discover why it used to be called the Coppersmith Shop when you pass under the **Shipbuilders and Engineers Sign (3).** This was the entrance to the old Wallace Shipyards, a complex with multiple industrial buildings and a workforce that peaked at 14,000 people during the Second World War.

Glance at the oversized photo of the workers of yesteryear leaving for the day and peruse the large sculptural recreation of hundreds of employment cards, showing their jobs and hourly pay rates. Then head around the end of the adjacent Pipe Shop building—now a pop-up event venue—before turning right along Wallace Mews.

You're now in **Shipbuilders' Square (4)**, a popular outdoor gathering place. But alongside the leafy trees, Adirondack chairs and seasonal ice rink (free with your own skates), there are multiple historic reminders. These include a towering old shipyard crane and lots of informative panels—including one about the 1,000 women who worked here during the Second World War.

Veer towards the water again and turn left along the shoreline until you reach **Burrard Dry Dock Pier (5).** Promenade along one of North Vancouver's favourite sunny day hangouts, stopping at the colourful four-part Indigenous mural that adorns the only building. Continue to the end of the pier and back, watching for cormorants en route.

Back on dry land, turn right and continue along the shoreline. It's quieter here, which suits the residents of the recently constructed condo towers. One of these developments curves around an old **Shipbuilding Berth (6)** that has been preserved for posterity. Look for the massive propeller—a remnant of a colossal navy ship that launched from here in 1944.

Nearby

- Park & Tilford Gardens (p. 112)
- Maplewood Flats (p. 111)

LYNN CANYON SUSPENSION BRIDGE

G&N

3663 Park Road, North Vancouver

Advising visitors to head to the free Lynn Canyon Suspension Bridge instead of the North Shore's paid suspension bridge attraction is a life hack locals love to flaunt. While this free bridge is not as tall or as long, stepping onto the swaying walkway with water thundering through the narrow canyon below is just as exhilarating.

You'll first arrive at the Lynn Canyon Ecology Centre, which you can visit for a suggested donation $2.00 per person or $5.00 per family. Otherwise, keep walking down the path towards the cafe and picnic area, passing interpretive signs detailing the history of the 250-hectare Lynn Canyon Park.

Continue down the steps and onto the 50-metre-tall crossing that was first hoisted in 1912. Stop at the halfway mark and admire the view of the waterfall below, where pristine turquoise waters rumble through the chasm.

Once across, you'll be among rainforest giants, with several trails winding through a network of boardwalks. We consulted the posted signs and headed south along the Baden Powell Trail to circle back over the Twin Falls Bridge. This loop is about 1.2 kilometres and includes plenty of stairs as the path dips past giant cedars, mossy maples and a fern-filled understory. Crossing back over Lynn Creek at Twin Falls, you'll be treated to more views of cascading waterfalls before you make your climb back up.

Freecouver Tip Ready to up your fitness game? As part of the international Parkrun movement, there are free Saturday morning 5-kilometre runs in West Vancouver, Vancouver, Richmond and Burnaby.

Nearby

- Cleveland Dam & Capilano River Regional Park (p. 107)

MAPLEWOOD FLATS

G&N

2649 Dollarton Highway, North Vancouver

You'll immediately feel connected to nature at this fantastic North Shore birding destination. But even if you don't have binoculars and the free Merlin Bird ID app, there is much to enjoy here. That starts near the entrance, where Ken Lum's *From Shangri-La to Shangri-La* sculptural installation recreates three 1940s squatters' cabins in miniature, including the home of novelist Malcolm Lowry.

Nearby, peruse the bird list outside the headquarters of the Wild Bird Trust, the non-profit that manages this unique conservation area. On our visit, killdeer, ospreys, red crossbills and dozens more had recently been sighted. Continue past the Coast Salish plant nursery (great for buying native BC plants) and the Corrigan Nature House, where free exhibits are often staged.

Next, glance at the trail map (available via the QR code) and start exploring the easy-access pathways that weave through the marshy, tree-lined terrain. On our visit, we soon spotted herons, red-winged blackbirds and several photogenic duck varieties. There are also lots of benches where you can sit and let the birds congregate around you—a simple but underappreciated spotting strategy.

Some of the best sightings here are along Burrard Inlet's mudflat shoreline, where we saw pintails, Green-Winged Teals and a Greater Yellowlegs noodling around. But since we were too early in the season for Maplewood's celebrated Purple Martins—they fly from South America to nest in dedicated bird boxes here—we immediately began planning an early summer return to catch them in action.

We'll also be back for the local Osprey Festival, a family-friendly August happening featuring local walks, live music, cultural demonstrations and much more.

Nearby

- Park & Tilford Gardens (p. 112)
- Freecouvering Around Lower Lonsdale (p. 108)

PARK & TILFORD GARDENS

G&N

333 Brooksbank Avenue, North Vancouver

Tucked into an inauspicious corner of North Vancouver's popular Park & Tilford shopping centre, this oasis-like, 1-hectare botanical garden is a delightful surprise. Created in 1969 by a local whisky distillery as a gift for the citizens of North Vancouver (and a handy promotional venue), it fell into ruin after the company collapsed in the early 1980s and before green-thumbed locals rallied to save it, preserving a celebrated attraction that in-the-know visitors love exploring.

Linked by winding pathways, it's divided into several themed horticultural areas. Most plants also have handy name plaques for easy identification. In the Herb Garden, you might spot everything from comfrey to meadowsweet to devil's tobacco. Whe Rose Garden—complete with an ironwork gazebo—is filled with plentiful fragrant varieties. There are also some towering, flowering trees to gaze up at, including a huge magnolia with creamy white blooms. The charming Oriental Garden, with its Japanese teahouse, curly-branched red maples and a perimeter wall topped with blue terracotta tiles, is the site's most photographed area.

Naturally, the time of year dictates the flowers you'll see during your visit. In spring, you might catch clematis or fawn lilies, while summer brings peonies and sea kale, for example. Whatever the season, there's always plenty to admire here, even in winter. That's when the annual, by-donation Hi-Light Festival takes place, adorning the garden with a sparkling tiara of festive illuminations.

Enthusiastically supporting the gardens are the FOGS (Friends of the Gardens Society). You'll often see these busy volunteers working away in the flowerbeds on Tuesday mornings from February to November.

Nearby

- Maplewood Flats (p. 111)
- Freecouvering Around Lower Lonsdale (p. 108)

WEST VANCOUVER ART MUSEUM

M&H

A&E

680 17th Street, West Vancouver

Donations are welcome but not required to visit this inviting two-room gallery tucked into a stone heritage house surrounded by a landscaped garden. Completed in 1939, it was originally the residence of teacher and artist Gertrude Lawson, one of the first women in BC to be given her own mortgage. Lawson, whose paintings were exhibited at the Vancouver Art Gallery and beyond, made her home a social and cultural hub for the community for many years.

That approach continues today at the art-and-design-focused museum now occupying the property. Staging four or five exhibitions throughout the year, you might see everything here from photos to video installations to works from the extensive permanent collection, which includes works by Lawson. Whatever you find, we recommend slowing down, reading the plaques and allowing yourself plenty of time to fully engage.

We also suggest timing your visit for one of the museum's free show-opening receptions, where you can chat with fellow art fans and meet a featured artist or two. And don't miss the gratis guided tours (typically in several different language editions) that bring to life the creations on the walls. Free family-friendly workshops, where kids can exercise their own artistic muscles, are also offered.

The museum's website points out these and other upcoming events. And it also provides updates on exciting plans to move the popular little museum to a much larger site over the coming years.

> **Freecouver Tip** Plot your own tour of North Vancouver's multitudinous public art with the city's downloadable Public Art Map.

Nearby

- Freecouvering Around the West Vancouver Waterfront (p. 114)

FREECOUVERING . . . AROUND THE WEST VANCOUVER WATERFRONT

A waterfront stroll with views of Stanley Park and downtown Vancouver, plus arts, culture and history—what's not to love? Begin your West Vancouver waterfront walk at the **Squamish Nation Welcome Figure (1)** in Ambleside Park. Welcoming all who pass the sandy shores with open arms, this 4.8-metre-tall carving is made from an old-growth

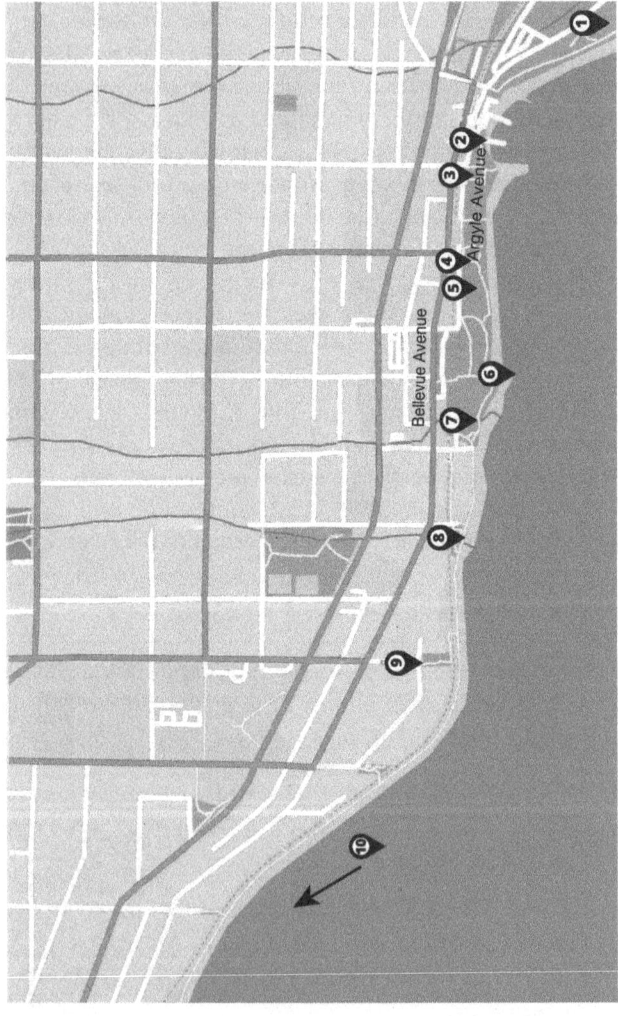

cedar log from Hollyburn Mountain and was a gift from the Sḵwx̱wú7mesh (Squamish) Nation.

Heading east, follow the beach over to the **Ambleside Fishing Pier (2)** where gulls hover above fishers casting their lines into the inlet. Enjoy views of cruise ships, windsurfers or wildlife, such as the occasional pod of Pacific white-sided dolphins or orcas passing through the first narrows. Stop in for a visit at the **Ferry Building Gallery (3)** at 1414 Argyle Street. For over a century, the Ferry Building has anchored cultural life in West Vancouver, first serving as a terminal for crossings to Vancouver and now as a community gallery with free admission.

Continue along the waterfront path to another free community exhibition space, the **Silk Purse Gallery (4)** at 1570 Argyle. It's right next door to the headquarters of the **Harmony Arts Festival (5)**. The festival hosts free events on the beach each summer that feature live music and a celebration of visual and culinary arts.

John Lawson Park (6) is your next stop, with its own pier, playground and a splash park for kids in the summer months. On the west side of the park you'll find historic **Navvy Jack House (7)** at 1768 Argyle Street, the earliest colonial dwelling west of the Capilano River, built circa 1872. It's currently being restored to preserve its heritage while adding community amenities. Back along the waterfront, the gravel path turns into the paved Centennial Seawalk, which will lead you past the **Seawalk Garden (8)**, designed as a peaceful retreat, then to Navvy Jack Point Park, tucked between private homes and featuring the ***Singsong Statue (9)***. This is a another tribute to John Thomas (Navvy) Jack, who developed the blend of sand, gravel and clay that bears his name and is still widely used in construction today. By the time you wrap up at **Dundarave Park (10)**, you've travelled almost 3 kilometres to another sandy beach, park space and pier. In winter, enjoy the free Dundarave Festival with Christmas Wassail and Bonfire, and the Forest of Miracles light display.

Nearby

- West Vancouver Art Museum (p. 113)

Tri-Cities

Coquitlam

Port Coquitlam

Port Moody

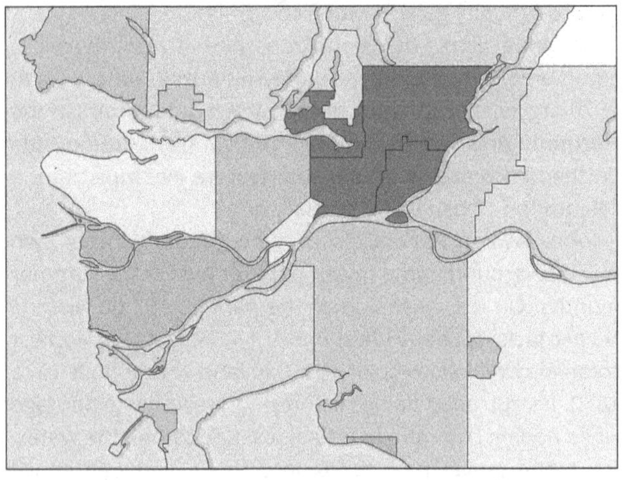

ART GALLERY AT EVERGREEN

A&E

1205 Pinetree Way, Coquitlam

A few steps from Lafarge Lake–Douglas Station at the end of the Millennium Line (Evergreen Extension), this small, white-walled gallery punches above its weight with a revolving array of intriguing contemporary art shows. Changing every quarter or so, you might find chin-stroking creations here by artists working in print, video, photography and much more.

Consider timing your visit for one of the free opening receptions, where you'll typically have the chance to meet and chat with the artists. Tours and additional events are also staged throughout each show's run, including popular family days when kids can create their very own works under friendly guidance. Most of these events are free or low-cost. We recommend registering ahead for family days.

Once you've perused the latest show—and also checked to see what's on at the excellent little theatre that shares the building—ask the front desk staff about any additional outdoor exhibits they are currently staging. Evergreen often curates installations at the nearby SkyTrain station, as well as around the outside of their own building, and these are always worth a selfie or two.

The gallery is also right next door to Town Centre Park, one of the region's favourite urban green spaces. When you visit, save time to stroll its pathways—bird-studded pond included—and consider returning to the area for the massive (and free) holiday light display, which takes over the park for several months every winter..

Town Centre Park typically hosts several major free events throughout the year, and these are well-worth timing your visit for. We especially recommend the Caribbean Days Festival in July.

Nearby

- PoCo Heritage Museum (p. 118)
- Riverview Tree Walk (p. 119)

POCO HERITAGE MUSEUM

M&H

A&E

2248 McAllister Avenue, Port Coquitlam

Tucked into Port Coquitlam's historic downtown, a few steps from the redbrick City Hall, this small community museum is a nostalgia-fest of local memories. Situated in a former post office building, it's home to an eclectic array of artifacts, each with a story to tell about what living here was like just a few decades ago.

Take your time noodling around the room (and reading the info panels), and you'll find everything from a milk delivery driver's hat to the hulking iron stove that heated the landmark Westminster Junction train station for many years. There's also a small fur-trimmed cape that May Day parade queens used to wear, alongside an album with photos of it in action back in the day.

Our favourite exhibit, though, is the large, cartoon-style mural depicting ducks outwitting hunters in several amusing ways. Created in the 1950s by Walt Disney artist Peter Carter-Page for the banquet rooms of PoCo's near-legendary Wild Duck Inn, it was rediscovered and saved just before the inn's demolition in 2008. It eventually found a home here when the museum opened in 2013.

The museum's website lists a lively roster of free events, along with a downloadable art walk map pinpointing local mosaics, installations and more. Speaking of art, the free Outlet Gallery is located right alongside the museum. It's one of several public gallery spaces in and around the surrounding Leigh Square area.

Outdoors, typically in August, the museum hosts the annual PoCo Car Free Day, a free, family-friendly street festival that includes live entertainment, games and activities, community booths and, of course, food.

Nearby

- Art Gallery at Evergreen (p. 117)
- Riverview Tree Walk (p. 119)

RIVERVIEW TREE WALK

G&N

Henry Esson Young Building,
Kalmia Place, Coquitlam

Step into the Serenity Gardens and sign-in with a volunteer for these free monthly tree tours offered from April to October (rain or shine) by the Riverview Horticultural Centre Society. The RHCS is dedicated to preserving and sharing the natural beauty of the historic gardens and sloping greenspaces of the former Riverview Hospital.

Set high above the Fraser River, the arboretum dates back to the hospital's opening in 1904. Since 1992, RHCS has offered tours of the 98-hectare səmiq̓ʷəʔelə (Riverview) site, which is managed by BC Housing in partnership with kʷikʷəƛ̓əm (Kwikwetlem) First Nation. Led by a botanist or arborist, tours are packed with insights and photo ops. You'll learn the difference between a sequoia cone and a cypress cone, or why Camperdowns Elms look the way they do. You'll soon be able to identify Paperbark maples, Japanese umbrella pines and Leopold maples. At one point, all 100 of us on the tour packed under the canopy of a giant weeping beech to marvel at nature's engineering. There's plenty of natural beauty to take in, from sniffing the foliage of a California incense cedar to catching a hint of magnolia on the breeze. It's a multi-sensory experience.

These walks help the Society spread awareness about preserving these aged trees while providing a delightfully entertaining day out in nature. With 1600 catalogued trees on the site, no two tours are ever the same in terms of what you'll see throughout the season, or depending on the specialty of your guide. From flowering double pink Kwanzan cherry trees in the spring, to the golden glow of Ginkgo biloba in the fall, the Riverview Tree Walk always delights. Dogs are welcome on a leash.

Nearby

- PoCo Heritage Museum (p. 118)
- Art Gallery at Evergreen (p. 117)

Multiple Locations

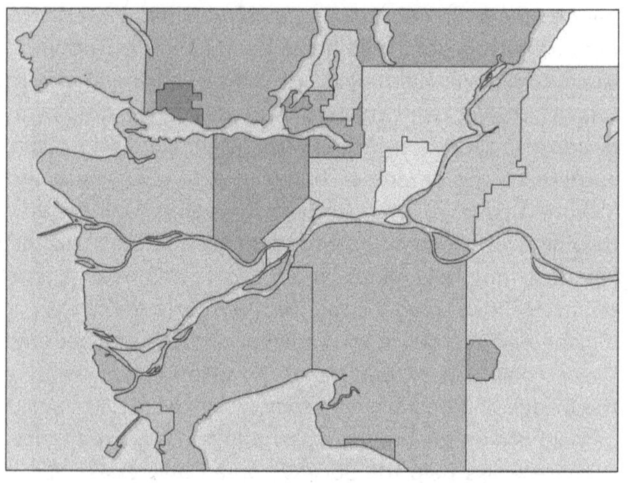

CHERRY BLOSSOM VIEWING

G&N

Vancouver & Various Locations

After a dark and dreary winter, there's nothing like a walk through the blossoms when spring arrives. Vancouver has more than 40,000 ornamental cherry trees at over 3,000 locations, featuring about 50 different cultivars. Over the past century, many of the city's trees have come from two key sources: gifts from Japan and a major Park Board planting initiative carried out between the 1960s and 1990s.

The season spans several months, starting in late February or early March, when the magnolias, alongside the purple Pissard plums, are the first pink blossoms to pop in downtown Vancouver. In late March and early April, the light and fluffy Akebono cherries form pillowy canopies that last for about two weeks before their petals shower down in light breezes, dusting the city in pink confetti. It's during this time that the Vancouver Cherry Blossom Festival hosts many free, public events, including picnics, walks and talks, and block parties. Some favourite spots to enjoy the blossoms include Stanley Park, Queen Elizabeth Park, David Lam Park in Yaletown, Garry Point Park in Steveston, and dozens of residential streets.

Finally, the deep pink clusters of the Kwanzan flowering cherry round out the season in late April. There's a noteworthy group of these trees in Coal Harbour, at the north end of Devonian Harbour Park. This cherry grove is the world's first-known AIDS memorial, planted in October of 1985.

Each of these cherry trees pulls double duty for photographers, offering one last show in fall, when their leaves trade green for fiery shades of orange and red.

Please keep in mind that these trees are delicate. Tempting as it is, refrain from pulling down branches or picking blossoms before they fall on their own.

WATERSHED TOURS

G&N

GFK

Coquitlam and North Vancouver

One of the easiest ways to access BC's breathtaking backcountry without triggering a rash of hiking blisters, these brilliant bus-and-walking tours are highly recommended. Visiting the pristine protected areas where our drinking water comes from, these nature-hugging excursions run throughout the summer—upcoming dates are posted in May and booking ahead is essential.

There are two main tours: one exploring the **Cleveland Dam & Capilano River Regional Park (p. 107)** and the other the Coquitlam watershed. A third tour covering the Lower Seymour Conservation Reserve is aimed at families and includes kid-friendly activities. We've taken both the Capilano and Coquitlam tours, and they are delightful days out filled with towering firs, snow-capped peaks and plenty of opportunities to spot wildlife.

After booking your chosen date—and gathering your sunhat, water bottle and appropriate footwear—you'll meet your guides at the designated pick-up point, a location easily reached by car or transit. After some preliminary info, you'll board the bus (typically a yellow school bus) and will soon be trundling along dusty gravel roads with the forest unfurling beside you.

En route, you'll learn fascinating facts about our water and how lucky we are to have such a great natural supply. You'll also stop at several clearings and scenic areas to walk around in the wilderness and snap as many photos as your phone or camera can handle—we especially love the panoramic shoreline views from the old water intake tower on the Coquitlam tour.

WILD BIRDS UNLIMITED BIRD WALKS

G&N

Around the Lower Mainland

If you're keen to try birding or you just want to join a group of like-minded enthusiasts for an outdoor stroll, these friendly and informative walks are excellent. Hosted by Wild Birds Unlimited, everyone's favourite local nature store, they're staged at different locations each month—past walks have included Blackie Spit, Trout Lake, Terra Nova Rural Park and more. Just remember to dress for the weather and bring binoculars and a water bottle.

On our morning walk, we met our avuncular guide and around 25 chatty participants in Queen Elizabeth Park's **Quarry Gardens** **(p. 35)**. We quickly learned how best to use our binoculars in conjunction with the free Merlin phone app that identifies birds via their sounds. This proved useful as we slowly walked the trails, listening for tweets and gazing intently into the branches of towering trees.

We soon spotted everything from ravens to ruby-crowned kinglets and from Anna's hummingbirds to red-breasted nuthatches. Some participants deployed telephoto lenses for great shots, but most of us simply enjoyed looking for slight movements in the foliage and pointing out discoveries to the group—while also communing with the natural world at a restoratively gentle pace.

Our expert guide answered many questions and led us to great areas throughout the park. And although we didn't see the tiny Pacific wren we were personally hoping to spot, we were delighted to see (or at least hear) a brown creeper, Cooper's hawk, several warbler varieties and some plump American Widgeons waddling around a pond like ungainly toddlers.